THE CULTURE FIX

THE CULTURE FIX

Bring Your Culture *Alive*, Make It *Thrive*, and Use It to *Drive* Performance

Will Scott

For general information about our products or services, please visit our website at https://www.cultureczars.com/, or contact the author at will@cultureczars.com.

Library of Congress Cataloging-in-Publication Data is on file with the publisher.

Publishers Cataloging-in-Publication Data
The Culture Fix: Bring Your Culture *Alive*, Make It *Thrive*, and Use It to *Drive* Performance by Will Scott
210 pages cm.
ISBN: 978-1-7348853-0-9 Paperback
978-1-7348853-1-6 ePUB
978-1-7348853-2-3 MOBI
978-1-7348853-3-0 Audiobook

Printed in the United States of America
Second edition

The following words and phrases found in this book are Trademarked or Registered by the author, Will Scott:

®

Culture Czars®

The Culture Fix®

™

Return on Culture™ (ROC)

CoreVals™

9 Deeds in 90 Days™

Alive, Thrive & Drive™

CorePurpose™

From Core Values to Valued Culture™

Core Workflow™

CoreChart™

CoreScore™

Unhired™

Entrepreneurial Operating System® (EOS) is a trademark registered by EOS Worldwide, LLC.

National Geographic® is a trademark registered by National Geographic Society

Dedication

Dedicated to Hugh and Shirley Scott
who initiated my values journey and to
Sam and Chloe Scott who will continue it.

Oh would some Power the gift give us,
to see ourselves as others see us.

—ROBERT BURNS

TABLE OF CONTENTS

Foreword

THE CULTURE OF A community, a country, a company, is its emotional lifeblood. It is an unseen force that guides and influences key interactions between people who keep businesses and organizations running. The tone and nuances of those interactions fuel the productivity of the employees, and thus the success of the company. Good chemistry and culture can bring great results to the bottom line, while a toxic environment can sink even the biggest company. Ignore developing a culture at your company's peril. Without a healthy culture, you won't be getting the best out of your business, your people, or your customers.

The impact of corporate culture is something I have witnessed throughout my executive career with BMW, Rolls-Royce, and Land Rover North America. These companies would not be the global behemoths they are without robust values. Strong cultures create strong brands. As a leader, it's not enough to hold personal values in your mind. They must be made memorable and lived daily in business processes and relations with teams and stakeholders. Consistent principles that are disseminated widely and pursued intentionally build foundations that underpin a business and a brand. Core values are fundamental components of creating worth and memorable customer experiences; without them, a business is unmoored and weakened. A strong living culture is essential for growth, value, and profit.

Well-defined and leveraged corporate culture is integral for outperforming competition. It is the single most important area of emphasis because it's the prioritization and the context that informs all decision-making. When the right people are working in a consistent direction, it enhances relationships within teams and with customers. In my decades of experience, one factor remains the same for all companies regardless of size or niche—people want to feel like they are part of something valuable. As a business or organizational leader, you have the opportunity to create this experience for your teams.

Though building culture seems abstract and therefore intimidates many business leaders, Will has created an accessible guide for taking core values and turning them into a valued culture. Within the pages of this book, you will learn how to take your own ephemeral values and turn them into a concrete culture that benefits every person who comes in contact with your business or organization. In breaking up the process into digestible, easily attainable steps, he is making it easier than ever for businesses and organizations to create strong cultures.

Using *The Culture Fix*, leaders will have the advantage to push their businesses and organizations to their fullest potentials. We are fortunate to have Will offer us his insights and guidance on going from simply having core values to truly turning a valued culture. I know this book will give readers the confidence and wisdom they need to become Culture Czars.

–Peter Miles, Former President of Rolls-Royce North America, Chief Operating Officer of BMW of North America, Executive VP of Land Rover North America, and Founder of Visionary Automotive Group, LLC.

Acknowledgements

I WOULD FIRST LIKE to acknowledge the people who will ultimately benefit from this book—employees everywhere who give of themselves every day to create, produce, serve, protect, deliver, and manage companies and organizations around the globe. Many of you are fortunate to work for organizations with great cultures where you can excel and contribute meaningfully to the world. You love where you work and why you work.

For others, however, you might not feel engaged at your workplace. Recent Gallup research shows that the majority of employees—51 percent—are disengaged and have been for quite some time: "Employee engagement has barely budged over the past decade and a half. From 2012 to 2016, employee engagement increased by just three percentage points. The U.S.—and the world at large—is in the midst of an employee engagement crisis."[1] I know from experience how challenging it is to dislike the working environment wherein you spend much of your time. My hope is that this book encourages you to become a Culture Czar and champion a change in your organization that will transform it into a place you value.

The U.S.—and the world at large—is in the midst of an employee engagement crisis.

1 Gallup, "State of the American Workplace," 2017.

I'd like to thank all the colleagues I have worked with in my companies including Waer Systems, Lextech Global Services, and Culture Czars. I acknowledge all the leaders and C-suite executives who understand that culture creates loyal employees, efficient teams, and higher growth and profitability. To those leaders who have invested in culture and deliberately nurtured it, thank you for caring and for providing great environments for your teams. I have learned so much from the leaders with whom I have partnered—especially Rod Scott, Nicki Scott, Alex Bratton, David Snelson, Peter Miles, and other fellow leaders in my own companies.

To my clients, *sawubona*—I see you. I am grateful for your deliberation and for the value you place on creating Culture Czars. Your Churchillian efforts have yielded admirable cultures, tremendous growth, and greater profitability for the companies you lead. The *abundancia* that you demonstrate daily is reflected in your families, your teams, your colleagues, and your customers. You truly are leading a culture, not just a company. I'd like to mention a few who particularly helped me bring this book to fruition: Kitsa Antonopoulos of Lumiere Children's Therapy; siblings David, Bob, Meaghan and Aimee of SABRE; Kevin Hundal of Atrend; Mike Stratta and Jake Hoover of Arcalea; Tim Heitmann of Double Good; and Chris and Brian of Matchnode.

Thanks to all the other business owners that I have been able to work with and who have contributed to this book and to my podcasts, many of them members of the Entrepreneurs Organization that has been so influential for me: Patricia Miller of Matrix4, Bejan Douraghy of Artisan Talent, Julie Mitchell of Torq Ride, Tim Padgett of Pepper Group, Linda Maclachlan of Entara, Todd Smart of Smart

Partners, Dan Heuertz of The Preferred Group, Erin Diehl of improve it!, Mike Petsalis of Vircom, Brian Waspi of Clear Water Outdoor, Dee Robinson of Robinson Hill, Lisa Scott of Scott Global Migration Law Group, Tony Mirchandani of RTM Engineering Consultants, Sonny Balani of Balani Custom Clothiers, and Rob Lindemann of Lindemann Chimney Company.

Writing a book is a herculean effort and a deeply personal process. It would not have been possible without the help of my patient, thoughtful editors Nancy Osa and Summer Flynn, my book designers Teddi Black and Susan Veach, and publisher team of Jade Maniscalco and Ben Allen of Tonic Books. I certainly could not have completed this task without the Culture Czars team of Jennifer Okray, Aalap Shah, Denton Heaney, Sam Scott, Jeremy Weiss, Cindy Zhu, and Regina Verdico. Credit for the amazing designs and much of the development of the Lextech core values story goes to Dao Yang, Cyril Wochok, and Erika Noble.

Lastly, I credit the brilliant thinkers and authors who have inspired me to grow, learn, and adapt into a culture-centric leader. I refer to, among others, Simon Sinek, Daniel Coyle, Daniel Pink, Jim Collins, Patrick Lencioni, Verne Harnish, and Gino Wickman.

Introduction

From Core Values to Valued Culture

Had I to good advice but listened,
I might, by this, have led a market,
Or strutted in a bank and clerked
My cash account:
While here, half-mad, half-fed, half-shirted,
Is all the amount.

—ROBERT BURNS, THE VISION

IT WAS "BEER-THIRTY" ON Friday afternoon at the Lextech offices. As president and integrator of one of the fastest-growing software companies in the country, I was in a fun mood, dressed in a black mask and shiny, dark cape. I was waiting in the conference room for my design team—or dream team, as they were known. We'd been using the weekly meeting to play Pictionary and brainstorm possible personas around our company's five core values, in order to bring them to life. We came up with a fictional band of superheroes based on our values that we dubbed *The Core*. On this afternoon, we'd be talking about our value of putting clients first.

The Core had quickly taken on a life of their own, and our staff took it upon themselves to gift me with a set of costumes, one for each core value character. The gesture showed that we were headed in the right direction. Thanks to the artistic talent of one of our designers, we also now had visuals to go along with our verbal character sketches. A cape-clad Captain Client led the team with his commitment to *clients coming first. Exude passion and energy* became Passionista, a can-do wonder of a woman. *Deliver success* was represented by Danny Deliver, a courier astride a cheetah. A buff Scotsman named Grow'n represented our commitment to strong *growth*, while invincible twins Tea and Wok demonstrated the epitome of *teamwork*. The personas added dimension to the words, while conveying our unspoken commitment to diversity. Many companies put their values into words, but ours had definitely taken on a new dimension. This took us several steps beyond simply having core value statements.

As we sat there, recalling the evolution of hunches into clearly defined sentiments, and phrases into full-color, larger-than-life superheroes, we felt the imperative of living the values they represented more strongly than ever. Bringing these bedrock goals into the company lexicon was showing us how powerful they could be. Our company's identity was evident to anyone who looked our way.

I witnessed this the night before from my seventeen-year-old daughter, Chloe. We'd been talking in the kitchen about a family friend's enthusiasm, when Chloe blurted out, "That's just what Passionista would do!" I was intrigued and asked her whether she knew what the persona stood for. *Passion and energy*, she quickly answered. Chloe had never worked a day at Lextech, and I wondered how many more of our core values she could recall. She suspected I was testing her, but obliged by naming every character and the value each represented. I was pleasantly surprised. I knew most employees in most companies could not name their own core values. Bringing them to life, as we had done with *The Core*, appeared to be a game changer.

Like my daughter, many people are visual learners. In fact, the Social Science Research Network, estimates that sixty-five percent of the population are visual learners.[2] Expressing concepts through imagery lets people connect to them emotionally and commit them to memory. The same is true for stories. Even without drawings, having characters put into story forms creates a context that helps people understand them. Stanford University's Robert E. Horn, best known for his development of information mapping, asserts that in our currently fragmented world, combining images with words is a powerful integration tool for groups and organizations:

> People think visually. People think in language. When words and visual elements are closely intertwined, we create something new and we augment our communal intelligence....Visual language has the potential for increasing human 'bandwidth,' the capacity to take in, comprehend, and more efficiently synthesize large amounts of new information. It has this capacity on the individual, group, and organizational levels.[3]

Wearing a mask and cape may seem a bit silly on the surface, however, my reasons for doing it were serious. As Horn's research has shown, I wanted my team to not only be aware of our company's core values, I wanted to integrate them into our communal experience. You can't just tell employees to *feel*

---

2 Bradford, William C., Reaching the Visual Learner: Teaching Property Through Art (September 1, 2011). The Law Teacher Vol. 11, 2004. Available at SSRN: https://ssrn.com/abstract=587201

3 Robert E. Horn, "Visual Language and Converging Technologies in the Next 10-15 Years (and Beyond)" (Paper presented at the National Science Foundation Conference on Converging Technologies for Improving Human Performance, Dec. 3-4, 2001).

something. You have to help them feel it. While core values mark the ideals by which you do business, living those ideals is the only way to show every member of the organization how earnestly you take them. The team and I certainly took them seriously, and as a result, Lextech grew 650 percent in just six years.

My first work experience was vastly different from the conference room of Lextech's 24,000 square feet of office space in Downers Grove, Illinois. My first job was on a farm in western England. Though it was a tough job that required working seven days a week for minimum wage and lodging, it was a valuable endeavor. I appreciated working amidst the daily rhythms of nature and caring for the animals. This was the time I started fully appreciating the writing of Scottish poet Robert Burns. Burns' poetry had always inspired me because of its reverence for the natural world. During my daily responsibilities on the farm, I felt akin to the ploughman poet in a new way. Like Burns, I was deeply engrossed in the natural rhythms of the world around me. I could see the profound magic held in the flora and fauna, the cycles of the animals, the erratic beauty of changing weather. What's more, I began to appreciate the message behind his poems, especially *The Vision*, which sought to preserve the dignity of Man. I understood on a new level that Burns was asserting that all men and women, regardless of occupation, were equal and worthy of respect. Though my responsibilities on this English farm were sometimes menial, like mucking out the barn, I understood what Burns was saying: my work still felt noble.

Furthermore, the farm owner had values that I easily related to and lived by every day. We were a great team, and I was totally committed to him, the farm, and its animals. I tirelessly worked long and hard days, yet my journals from the time record my deep satisfaction with my life and chosen endeavor. I imbued the pride that I thought Burns spoke of in his poem, "Strive in thy humble sphere to shine." Furthermore, I felt confident in this job. I remember understanding my supervisor's priorities and what to do when the unforeseen occurred. Although it might not have been glamorous, the farm was a successful business, and one could tell just by seeing the way it was cared for.

A year later, I worked on a different farm as a part of my schooling and had a wildly contrasting experience. There was little direction and discipline, poor leadership, and no sense of values, or at least none that I related to. The result was chaos. Workers were not aligned and there was high turnover. Oftentimes, workers would just stop showing up. Many didn't seem to take any pride in their work. I realized that I had lost the dignity that Burns spoke of—not because the type of job changed, but because something more ephemeral was missing. The contrast was obvious and stuck with me. I decided then to maintain a determined path toward dignified work environments, because they can drastically affect the way one feels about work, and ultimately, one's self.

This lesson stayed with me as I finished college and worked toward an MBA. With each job that I held in the interim, I saw how a leader's values affected his/her workforce. After finishing business school at the University of Southern California, I worked for a privately-owned American company with the challenge of expanding their export markets overseas.

This company was void of values and structure, and when the management team asked the owner for direction, little was given. It was easy to fail and hard to succeed because no one knew what attainment looked like. Noble initiatives to bring progress or success to the organization were criticized to the point that innovations were stifled. Without directions or goals, there were no ideal behaviors, conflict resolution, or overall purpose. Those who risked the least survived because it was an environment that was disinterested in change and lacked any sense of teamwork or cooperation. Today I know that core values and a core purpose would have helped the environment immensely, but at the time, I tolerated the lack of a defined culture alongside my coworkers.

Not long after, my brother Rod presented me with the opportunity to start a new company—a spin-off from his aerospace component distribution business with some brilliant logistical concepts at its core. In 1999, we started Waer Systems. As a small team we built amazing software that has run mission critical supply chain operations for companies like Airbus and Bombardier for much of our twenty-year history. We evolved as technology and markets changed, and in the last few years made a pivot to being a Built for Oracle Net Suite partner, specifically in the Warehouse Management space. We now have installations in many different industries all over the world and are adding new customers at a rapid pace. I learned about working with family too, which had its own particular joys and challenges. (This experience would prove invaluable as I later assisted family-owned companies with their cultures.) Together my brother and I rode the highs and lows of closing deals with billion dollar companies, raising millions of dollars in venture capital funding, managing boards of directors, struggling with cash flow, and all the other challenges of a small start-up. Nevertheless, we never missed an opportunity to celebrate, and we never lost sight of our familial and individual values.

At Waer Systems, I started thinking a lot about the environment of a work place. Not just the physical space, but something intangible that manifested in tangible results—happy employees, less turnover, more efficient teams. I thought back to my work on the farm. I recalled that the most important precursor to a bountiful harvest came months before with the cultivation of the soil and the planting of the seeds. Cultivating the soil was a tending period that happened before the harvest. I saw firsthand that taking the time to nurture the soil had a direct correlation with the health and success of the crop.

From the disparate work experiences of my youth and early adulthood, I recalled that whether I was on a farm or in a conference room, the cultural environment made a direct impact on my satisfaction and success. In fact, the word *culture* comes from the Latin word *cultura,* meaning to grow or cultivate, and was often used in reference to the care of soil. I realized that taking this principle off of the farm and into the workplace could produce the same results.

With this in mind, I thought about Waer Systems. I wanted to develop the culture so that we could reap lasting benefits in the future. What was interesting was that although we were a geographically diverse team, our core values and defined culture helped us operate effectively, even though we were operating on three continents. Twenty years later, this company continues to flourish, and many of our initial employees are still thriving with us.

After building a culture based on values at Waer Systems, I was eager to try the same process again. In 2010, I partnered with Alex Bratton in Lextech, a mobile app software development company. This is where I honed the corporate culture experiences I share in the following pages. It became a fast-growing and successful company with core values and attention to culture at its foundation.

Helping struggling, divided corporate cultures transition to successful, united companies through the application of effective core values is what led me to design and offer the 9 Deeds in 90 Days workbook to other companies as part of my Culture Czars program. In 2016, I became a consultant and business system implementer to other fast growing entrepreneurial companies, and I continue to see how the program leads to more successful companies with more fulfilled and dedicated work forces.

Now, let me ask: What's the toughest conversation you've had to initiate as a business leader? Was it with management colleagues over setting a course for the future? Maybe it was with human resources personnel about letting someone on the staff go? Or, more seriously, have you had to lead a significant downsizing? Whatever the topic, it probably wasn't the first tough talk you've had, and it definitely won't be the last. Difficult conversations stir negative emotions, which often get in the way of doing business. Corporate executives, supervisors, and anyone with the title of "boss" feel the pain that surrounds emotive issues—or issues that people take personally—more deeply than the rest of the world might think. It's not because every one of us is thin-skinned; it's because we know we'll be spending inordinate amounts of time on thorny issues that carry emotional baggage rather than attending to more relevant concerns. Furthermore, if the matter is left unaddressed the issue will fester and gnaw away at our subconscious. People problems detract from business operations and bear large costs in time, money, and worry. You may not be able to fix other people's problems, but you can change the environment into a healthy workplace culture that supports and addresses personal and professional matters.

Focusing on culture, on the other hand, eliminates ineffective patterns, sets a more positive course, and then *perpetuates that course* all on its own. That's the beauty of leading a culture instead of just leading a company.

To build or rebuild your company's culture, you must make a similar priority—you have to put culture above all else. However, most business leaders don't think in terms of "culture first." It's hard not to get caught up in internal issues, recurring problems, and glitches in what you thought were proven strategies. In addition, there are market shifts, Human Resources (HR) trends, and other external factors that can mentally drain a leader. Trying to wrestle with these concerns piecemeal will only cause repetition of the issues. Focusing on culture, on the other hand, eliminates ineffective patterns, sets a more positive course, and then *perpetuates that course* all on its own. That's the beauty of leading a culture instead of just leading a company. With a little preventive care and maintenance, healthy cultures run autonomously, leaving you free to focus more on growth and the big picture. When you put off those difficult-yet-necessary conversations because just thinking about them gives you a queasy feeling in your gut, your core values will guide you and empower your dialogs. They will strengthen your ability to step into a room and have that talk go a lot more smoothly. Later in the book, I'll show you how to plan and execute such conversations by referencing your core values.

No matter the number of employees, the diversity of the group, or their location, by putting culture first, a leader's job is made easier. Many CEOs start out with a grand vision for the future, only to become trapped in day-to-day details. This might be a metaphor for the world at large. Our global society is so segmented and concerned with petty issues that our human potential is barely realized—leaving the majority of individuals feeling unfulfilled.

In a 2018 study by Mercer, called the Global Talent Trends Study, they received input from 800 business executives, 1800 Human Resources professionals, and more than 5,000 employees from 21 industries across countries. With almost 8,000 people surveyed, the study determined 3 factors that create a successful and efficient workforce: workplace/schedule flexibility, commitment to health and well-being, and working with a purpose. In fact, the study showed that employees were 3 times more likely to work for a company with a strong sense of purpose.[4] The Culture Czars program may not be a panacea for all that is implied here, but it will certainly provide many of the key pieces that will ensure your employees are cared for in these three important areas of workplace satisfaction.

---

4 Mercer, "Mercer Global Talent Trends 2018 Study," https://www.mercer.com/our-thinking/career/global-talent-hr-trends.html#.

We have the cure—we simply have not made administering it a priority. What if we did? If the world were an enterprise, and if it adopted the techniques known to strengthen culture—such as building trust and establishing open communication—then many personal problems would melt away. Our teams would find the purpose they are desperately seeking in work environments and the world would function efficiently, with workers knowing their purpose, being empowered to pursue it, and getting better at what they do.

I believe this is possible on a global scale because I have seen it work on an individual business scale. Even as a child, I sensed that being intentional about culture would produce an environment where everyone had the opportunity to reach their potential, or at least reach *for* it. My lifelong attraction to creating environments where people thrive eventually prompted me to make it my life's work. Now I offer this methodical approach toward attaining a truly value-added culture.

How I Became a Culture Czar

We all begin to shape our personal values through trial and error when we are young. We innately gravitate toward certain passions and priorities, even though they may not make sense at the time. I grew up in Zambia surrounded by the natural rhythms of life. Many of the lessons I learned were surmised from my observations of the world around me, helped by my father whose love of nature and the outdoors was infectious. One value he passed to me was a love of trees, including Africa's iconic baobab trees. I recall riding through the bush with my father as we guessed how many hundreds or even thousands of years each tree had existed. Known as "the tree of life," the baobab trees provided shelter and nutrition for humans and animals. The most interesting feature was the tree's ability to withstand drought. Inside its massive trunk, it stored hundreds of liters of water that could help it survive even the harshest drought conditions. Not only did the tree have the capacity for self-preservation, it could also be tapped and used to satiate humans and animals alike. These massive symbols of timelessness, reliability, stoicism, protection, and selflessness later came to represent one of our core values at Culture Czars. Eucalyptus and mango trees grew in our backyard and they became places where I fulfilled an early passion: building clubhouses in trees. These spaces always had rules, or as we call them in the corporate world, values.

Whether it was a treehouse, a fort on stilts, underground cave dwelling, or sophisticated bamboo hut under a mango tree, there was one constant: people to gather in them. I would create these little, enclosed worlds and invite my friends to share them. Anywhere people gathered, though, there was potential for drama, friction, jostling for power, selfish motives, and contentious points of view. It was important to me, having put the effort into creating these environments, that my friends didn't trash them, disrespect them, or of course, reveal their locations. So, I set rules and posted them—much like the popular posters of core values that you'll see in many of today's businesses—to keep us all on the same page. I decreed: *No littering; Be nice; Keep this place secret*; and, of course, *No adults "aloud."* Little did my peers know, those early experiences foretold my life's mission: *to create environments where people thrive.* Even at that formative age, I was defining my role as a potential Culture Czar—a leader who strives to exemplify a group's core values.

One of my early forts complete with retractable ladder, circa 1970

Looking back, I realized that posting fort rules was part of establishing bonds with my friends. We were in an exclusive club, bound by our agreed-upon policies. We knew what the boundaries were, how to interact, and ultimately, how each person could be a successful member. This also created a common experience for my visitors and guaranteed the most fun for the most people. Was it also a little bit controlling? Or was I inadvertently setting myself up as a leader who was ready to take responsibility for the group's well-being? Probably both. The rules kept me—club president and peer—from having to constantly police my friends. Instead of grumbling about picking up trash, I could just point to the sign and say, "We all agreed not to litter." Done. Short conversation, no argument, everyone felt better. Furthermore, if friends were being mean to each other, I could simply remind them, "We agreed to be nice." I didn't have to reprimand, cajole, or teach during awkward moments of conflict. All I had to do was refer to a standard that we understood and were committed to.

Only later in my life did I fully understand the impression that my early structures had on my life. In creating dynamic environments for my friends, I wasn't just building forts. I was communing with these "trees of life" that served as powerful reminders that a cultivated foundation was essential for strong growth. Even in drought conditions, the trees endured, not because of what they displayed externally, but because they had a rooted, unshakable core that could provide the sustenance they—and their communities—might one day need. In many ways, these trees, and the forts and structures I built among them, were my earliest lessons on how to build healthy communities and cultures.

Why Invest in Culture?

At a Young Presidents Organization (YPO) event in Chicago several years back, I had the opportunity to share my Culture Czars mission with Simon Sinek, author of *Start with Why*. His response was, "That's great; but why?" I should have known this would be his retort. I replied, "So they can be the best that they can be." And he said, "That's better." What began as "creating environments where people thrive" was completed as "so that they can be the best that they can be." My life's mission suddenly had a purpose, and I was lucky enough to have it crafted, in part, by the best in the business! As I have come to understand the value of living a life aligned to one's purpose and knowing the power one feels from it, I have tried to define this purpose even further. This led me back to the poetry of Robert Burns. As I mentioned, I had been drawn to Burns' reverence for the natural world ever since I worked on a farm. Thinking on it with my realized "why" in mind, I began to see my connection to Burns as something much deeper—it wasn't just the natural world he lauded; it was the plight of the common man that he extolled. Each of his poems, including *The Vision*, resonated with me because it celebrated equality. I realized that from the time I was a boy building forts, I too had sought parity among my peers. I wanted to create spaces where all were welcomed and equal.

That's the "why" of The Culture Fix—to stick up for employees so that they might love where they work and why they work. I want men and women to leave their jobs feeling good about their day's work, whether that is on a farm in England or in a C-suite office in NYC. No matter the work, each day is an opportunity to appreciate the joy of work alongside others and to make meaningful contributions to the world. Reading through *The Vision* with this concept in mind, I realized why Burns' vision for the culture at large resonated with me so much. We want a culture that is inclusive, connected, and steeped in values. For this reason, Burns' poem *The Vision* has continued to inspire my "why" and is the reason you will see stanzas of its modern English translation reprinted throughout the book. Though the original Scottish dialect can be cumbersome, the ideas behind the words inspire me daily to contribute to the wider culture by cultivating the cultures of as many companies as possible.

What my conversation with Sinek helped confirm for me is that believing in a concept is the start, but naming it is powerful too. Just as my innate drive for inclusivity was just a jumble of unrealized beliefs before I invoked it verbally, so a company's values are merely concepts until they are fully actualized. How does one make these concepts into fully actualized core values? Through *The Culture Fix* and its 9 Deeds in 90 Days.

Why culture? It's simple—no other initiative brings greater rewards for all members of a team. For the price of some teamtime and a few bucks in printing, developing culture:

- Requires a low capital investment
- Produces the highest return
- Is one of the most rewarding experiences you can have alongside your team

We'll talk more about tangible return on investment (ROI) in later chapters. You may be a hard-driving CEO who cares about results, but it's okay to have some fun and feel good about it. Not only is it okay, your team will love you for it, stay with you longer, and give you more. Now, that's a healthy environment in which people desire to work.

Healthy cultures make companies thrive. Companies with broken cultures merely survive, or even fail. What's the cultural difference between thriving versus surviving? In survival mode, resources are stretched thin, staff are stressed out, employees leave, while replacements stall performance and cost money. The trickle-down effect soon hits your customer base. Furthermore, clients can sense the desperation of survival mode. As Julie Mitchell, founder and CEO of Torq Ride, shared with me in an interview for the Culture Czars podcast series *From Core Values To Valued Culture* (see the Products and Services page at the end of book for a link to our podcast series), culture affects every facet of a company, from employee fulfillment to client satisfaction:

> [Culture is] the feeling or the experience that you have when you interact with the brand. And I don't see it as something that's limited to the employees of a company. I think the culture lives in the experience that the customers are having as well....I really think about the culture as something that works regardless of who the audience is—whether it's the suppliers that you're working with, the staff, or the customers—they're all part of that culture experience.

Cultures fail, or lose their authenticity, when their underpinnings are forgotten. One company that is often lauded for its culture is Southwest Airlines, which has grown into the country's most successful airline. Much of the company's success began with Co-Founder Herb Kelleher's leadership style that gave employees input in decision making. With an emphasis on Southwest's people, Kelleher advised, "Orient your mission statement in terms of how you want to treat your internal and external customers. That makes it both meaningful and eternal...if you focus on your people, your mission statement is eternal."[5]

Maybe Southwest's focus on people began with the idea of having a fun-loving attitude, but it's clear the values established in the beginning have persevered throughout four decades of unparalleled success in the airline industry. They had leaders who understood that putting culture first—which is really putting employees first—pays off in extremely valuable ways. Hiring better "fits" improved performance, retention, and greater transparency. This resulted in higher functioning teams and more accountable staff. These intangible improvements produced real results like fewer recruitment headaches, less office drama, and superior work outcomes, which ultimately translated into better revenues and happier people who were excited to come to work.

Your investment is largely a matter of commitment. You commit to doing some honest thinking, to carving out time to get the process in place, and to making a modest financial investment. These will soon be repaid with exponential returns. You'll see gains associated with higher productivity, better customer relations, and stronger employee attendance and retention to name a few. There's no need to take a class, get certified, or be an expert in anything other than what you are already doing. It all hinges on identifying and articulating your values.

Any smart business makes investments in its greatest assets, so if you believe people are your greatest asset, com-

---

5 *How Southwest Airlines built its culture,* YouTube video, 5:35, posted by World of Business Ideas, October 20, 2016, https://www.youtube.com/watch?v=8_CeFiUkV7s&feature=youtu.be.

mit to it. Investing in culture *is* investing in your people. It lets you use them to their best advantage and full potential. Bringing culture alive in this way helps people thrive—so they can drive your business to the top.

> Investing in culture *is* investing in your people. It lets you use them to their best advantage and full potential.

Results You Can Expect

Imagine how easy it would be to get your staff involved in culture if you told them they could:

- Work for more than just a paycheck
- Know that their personal traits are valued because you hire employees for how well they will fit in with the group
- Increase their job security by knowing what success in their role looks like
- Be empowered to make decisions by using core values as guidelines
- Be part of something greater than one person or one company

Besides knowing that you are responsible for those specific benefits, you can expect big personal and professional changes from your new culture-first mindset. Not only will you see the changes in the contentment of your workforce, you will also find that you are leading a more competent and united team, thus making your own schedule and workload more streamlined and efficient.

As the leader of a culture-first team, you'll be able to:

- Give tough conversations finite boundaries and clear-cut resolutions
- Educate and empower employees to make decisions in line with values, rather than having to delegate or authorize individual actions
- Free up your time for executive duties by relying on qualified staff members
- Be more accurate and successful at hiring for cultural fit
- Give your clients something to believe in

As Simon Sinek said, "People don't buy what you do, they buy why you do it."[6] Using the foundations I have honed during my own experience as a corporate leader, I offer the same perspective and framework to other leaders. It doesn't matter what type or size of your company or organization, I have seen the 9 Deeds in 90 Days initiative benefit small businesses and large corporations alike. Here's how you can use what you are reading *right now* to become a Culture Czar—a leader who exemplifies a company's core values—and jump-start your company's cultural initiative.

Learn the lingo. If you're a student of culture and business writing in general, you're familiar with the usual clinical terms: core values, mission and vision, and employee evaluations. Executives use them over and over, and the terms

6 *Start with Why*, YouTube video, 18:01, posted by TEDx Talks, September 28, 2009, https://www.youtube.com/watch?time_continue=2&v=u4ZoJKF_VuA.

tend to drown out the message behind them. I'm a big fan of memorable catch phrases, so I incorporate some concepts in my own shorthand expressions. Below is a list of the terms you will see used in the following chapters.

Culture Czars Glossary

CoreVals: a company's core values.

CorePurpose: the overarching company goal and reason for being.

CoreWorkflow: the overarching company workflow or master process.

CoreChart: an infographic that combines a company's CoreVals, CorePurpose, and Core-Workflow.

CoreScore: a numeric measurement that indicates the degree to which employees and teams work in concert with CoreVals.

Core People Processes: the hiring, unhiring, and evaluating protocols based on CoreVals.

Culture Czar: a leader who exemplifies a company's CoreVals and a champion of the corporate culture.

Get the big picture. Each chapter includes a brief discussion of why and how to take another step toward a more intentional culture. You've probably already done your homework, so you'll see less data and statistics and more practical advice. The 9 Deeds will help you break down the big picture into manageable snapshots.

9 Deeds

- Discover
- Discern
- Describe
- Design
- Decree
- Dictate
- Devise
- Deliver
- Determine

Drill down to the details. Each chapter ends with a workbook exercise. Give thought to each of these sections on your own, with much introspection and the kind of attention you'd give your most pressing issues, and then complete the exercise with your team. Each exercise will build on the one before it and by the end of the exercises, you will have a cultural plan ready to implement with your team.

Take it one week at a time. Rome wasn't built in a day, and neither was Roman culture. Invest the time and effort, and it will pay off. The Culture Czars process is a specific system that is easy to learn and implement. One nice thing about working with values and culture is that you can fit these tasks into your weeks at your convenience, although you have to really consider culture-building as part of your job description and schedule the work. You can comfortably accomplish each Deed around your other company demands. Even if you have to miss one week, you can still complete the entire program within 90 Days. In just one calendar quarter, you'll be closer to having a truly valued culture. Warning: This is addictive and fun! The more time you devote to the effort, the more you will want to do. Then you'll know you're a Culture Czar.

PART ONE:

ALIVE

Bring Your Core Values to Life

- ✓ Discover
- ✓ Discern
- ✓ Describe

CHAPTER 1

Discover

Her mantle large, of greenish hue,
My gazing wonder chiefly drew;
Deep lights and shades, bold-mingling, threw
A lustre grand;
And seemed, to my astonished view,
A well-known land.

—ROBERT BURNS, THE VISION

YOU ARE A CEO, a company founder, a department head, or some other brand of business leader. You set the tone for your employees. This is a buck you cannot pass. Many times, when I see a broken company culture, it's because the person at the top is not living by example. Hypocrisy doesn't forward your agenda. Remember that values are connected to emotions. If you don't emotionally engage your team, they will have no reason to feel or act on those values.

The thought of emotionally engaging with a group leaves some leaders in a panic. However, connection can be quite simple. All great company cultures start at the top with excellent leadership. Simply put, you can't have one without the other. Before we can get into the Culture Czars program, we must first make sure the team leader lives the values the company hopes to imbue. From my consulting work with many corporate leaders, I have found that the most successful leaders are the ones who share the following five traits:

1. They have a "culture-first" mentality: If you're someone else's boss, it's hard not to get caught up in the day-to-day internal and operational problems. Nevertheless, great Culture Czars create space to focus on culture, invest time to create core values (which we refer to as CoreVals), and spend energy to bring them alive and make them thrive. They realize that focusing on culture ultimately eliminates the ineffective patterns that can easily bog them down. They understand that creating a valued culture sets a more positive course. In short, their mission is much grander—they see themselves as leading a culture, not just a company.

2. They're closely involved with the people operations: Successful Culture Czars take ownership of the people side of business. The number one thing that influences your culture is the people—Culture Czars don't hand-off critical people operations to someone else. They are constantly involved in assessing and managing, making sure the people working within the organization are the right fit. Cultural fit is a key part of hiring decisions, and when an employee is a drain on the culture, they take steps to quickly unhire him/her.

Linda Maclachlan, CEO of Entara, an IT managed service firm, takes this seriously. Empathy is one of Entara's CoreVals and she begins laying the framework the minute employees come on board. In an interview with her for the Culture Czar podcast series, she laughed and said, "I'm probably the only leader on the planet who has their technical engineers watch a Brené Brown [expert on vulnerability in leadership] video about the meaning of empathy. That is how we start our new employee training." What Maclachlan understands is that core values are not an afterthought; they are an integral, foundational piece to introduce as soon as possible.

3. They champion the CoreVals internally and externally: Great Culture Czars take every opportunity to discuss their CoreVals and share stories about the company culture on every public stage—at company-wide meetings, at speeches outside the organization, even during engagements with partners. As we will discuss fully in later chapters, they tell stories to ensure they become a part of company folklore. They're proud of the culture they have worked hard to cultivate, and they help make it thrive by sharing current examples of how the culture positively shapes their workplace.

4. They really *see* their employees: As I mentioned in the Introduction, I spent my childhood in Southern Africa and there is a Zulu greeting there, *sawubona*, meaning "I see you." As a full acknowledgment of a person's presence, it's a wholehearted recognition of the total person in front of you and what he or she brings to the world. That's different than the typical "hi" we mutter when greeting our colleagues in the office. *Sawubona* suggests a moment of actual connection—something that our usual greetings tend to lack. Even beyond a simple acknowledgement, we rarely *see* each other in the workplace. Leaders especially, should take the time to fully recognize the people they work with each day. It's a small thing that can make a big difference in elevating company culture, and it's a good place to start for a burgeoning Culture Czar. Even if people don't remember what you said or did, they will surely remember how you made them feel.

> Even if people don't remember what you said or did, they will surely remember how you made them feel.

As a leader, when you see an employee you haven't seen in a while, take sixty seconds to offer more than a passing "hello." Make eye contact and take the time to be fully present. I actually linger with my handshake—I hold on a second longer and sometimes clasp my other hand over the back of their hand in a more sincere, two-handed grip. It sounds a bit awkward when described this way, yet you're doing this with the intention of wanting to *know* and *see* the other person.

A greeting is a moment to create a meaningful connection, if we use it that way. Apart from the individual effect, it creates a solid foundation for a great culture. Bejan Douraghy, CEO of the staffing agency Artisan Talent and fellow Culture Czar, created a company that *sees* its employees as well as its clients. When I interviewed him for the podcast series, Bejan explained that empathy—understanding and sharing what another person is feeling or experiencing—is a leading CoreVal, central to everything they do. Empathy is so critical for Bejan, who started Artisan Talent thirty years ago, that he actually refers to himself as "Chief Empathy Officer." He sees empathy as a "differentiator" of how employees behave internally, how they treat the talent they source, and how they work with their clients. "When I look back, why did I leave a company and start my own? [Because] it really wasn't a cultural fit for me," he says, adding that he intuitively knew he wanted to create a business that recognized the person. "Of course, sales targets and key performance indicators (KPIs) are important," he says, "but you're unlikely to get there if you don't create a culture that fosters more than just numbers. If you have the right people in place, if you have the right culture in place, those numbers will follow. You really need that human element."

Once a leader is confident with the team they have built, they must continue to cultivate those relationships. They show up and take opportunities to connect with them. They're concerned with those one-on-one interactions and know that taking a moment to meaningfully connect with the people they work with can go a long way. It makes employees feel like they're at the right place, working with the right people.

5. They recognize their culture champions: Leaders who value culture recognize and reward employees who act in accordance with the CoreVals. The marketing agency Pepper Group exemplifies this with their "kick-ass awards," a peer-to-peer recognition program. Colleagues nominate each other for stand-out behavior—it could be as simple as coming in early or helping out a teammate with a project.

Pepper Group Kick-Ass Award

Pepper nominated: ______________________

By: ______________________

On: ______________________

For: ______________________

____

____

And demonstrating one or more of the following Core Values:

- ○ Initiative has no Boundaries
- ○ Work & Play with Passion
- ○ Pride in Craft & Service
- ○ Be Smarter Tomorrow
- ○ Scraped Knees Teach Us to Dance
- ○ Face to Face with Grace
- ○ Strength of the Wolf is in the Pack
- ○ Choose to be Challenged

If you need more room to describe reason—write smaller.
Self-nominated Nominees will get their Ass-Kicked.
Nominations will be voted upon by a Panel of Prestigious Pepper Personnel.
Not to be confused with the "What-An-Ass" Award.

The Pepper Group's Kick-Ass Award Nomination Form

"We don't really have definitions for what a kick-ass behavior is, because I think it's personal," Pepper Group Founder and CEO, Tim Padgett, explained on the Culture Czars podcast. "Whoever thinks someone kicked-ass, that's good enough for us, and we don't measure [employees] against each other."

The Pepper Group's peer-to-peer recognition program reads submissions aloud every week at the company-wide meeting.

All the submissions are read out loud every Monday morning at the company-wide meeting. Employees really like to start the week on this note. Even though they're just a team of seventeen, Tim says there are around 15-30 submissions each week. There's no financial reward for these—just an aptly named trophy. The public recognition and reinforcement are enough incentive as evidenced by the ongoing enthusiastic participation.

In recognition of an employee's hard work, the Pepper Group gives out the "Kick Ass" award each week.

As we will discuss fully in the following chapters, making these small changes in how you interact with your team sets the right foundation for the culture you will build. Just as the CEOs referenced above created cultures around their team values, you will also create your own customized work culture based on the values that pertain to your business and your mission. We'll start the program by bringing your core values to life and mapping out an action plan by answering these questions:

- Who decides on company values? Just you? A few senior VPs? Your full management team?
- How will you sketch out these values? Over lunch, meetings, or a retreat?
- Who do you think your Culture Czars will be? What will you ask of them?
- How will you be the greatest Culture Czar of all and the most aligned with the CoreVals?

When I ask my consulting clients what they've learned from building culture, they say they appreciate the contemplation and emotional honesty involved. Many entrepreneurs do not consider these ephemeral concepts part of their official duties or even their skill sets. The truth is, everybody has the capacity for deep thought and self-discovery, some just don't respect the so-called softer aspects of running a business—or they believe people won't respect them if they do.

Dan Heuertz, CEO of The Preferred Group, spoke during a Culture Czar podcast of the role emotional intelligence should play in the workplace:

> For some reason in business, we're told not to talk about our feelings. Like they're separate, put them in a box and never take them out. But what I learned...was that the more emotionally intelligent you are, the greater results you'll get as a leader and as a CEO....There's such a thin line today between personal and professional. It's so thin. I blur those lines every day. I'm not even sure if there is a line anymore. But if there is, and let's assume there is for a minute, it's so thin that if you're going to be your true self all the time, then feelings and emotions are part of who you are as a human being. I don't know how you get away from it.

Bejan Douraghy, also understands the power of leading with emotions, especially empathy. In a podcast, he explained how these softer sides of leadership are powerful tools for his team's successes:

> It's a particular process that we have interviewees go through. And the characteristics that we're looking for, the cultural characteristics that we've defined, are smart, caring, nurturing, creative, and driven. Those are the key values that we are striving to find. You're not going to get it with everyone, but those are the ones that we are looking for, and you can hire for that....I think more and more companies are going to be [leading with emotions]. They have to if they want to survive with the newer generations of people that are more in touch with their feelings, more in touch with their emotions and the cultural fit.

I completely agree with Bejan and Dan and feel that more leaders are reassessing the value of emotions in the work place. When I hear leaders who traditionally shy away from such matters, I ask, "Isn't the way your team feels when they are at work with you—in the environment you control—of consequence?" Considering they are your most important assets and the greatest drivers of your company's success, you know the answer to that one.

The Creative Process at Work

Are you guilty of believing that you have to be typing, in meetings, or on the phone in order to get things done? Then put aside any skepticism and try thinking about the culture that you want to deliberately define and bring to life. Set aside chunks of time for the thought processes requested in this chapter. When that works out, do it for the next chapter. Even if you're pressed for time now, once your culture is alive and well, you'll appreciate the investment and find more minutes for thought in your workday.

For many businesses I have consulted with, there is already a theme or mantra that drives the decision-making. This can be a helpful starting point when thinking of core values. Culture Czar Bejan Douraghy shared with me the simple theme that has served him well in his tenure at Artisan Talent

> [We] came up with a phrase that explains what we do and explains our culture and that phrase for us is: *inspiring better lives*....We wanted to really bring it down to one phrase and that, of course, was not easy. But for us it's about inspiring better lives.... How are we doing that for our clients? How are

> we doing that for the talent that we represent? And then how are we doing it internally?...It's hard to get it that simple, but you've got to get it to the point where all your employees don't need a big message....Just start with a phrase—inspire. Inspire what? *Inspire better lives.*

Dan Heuertz uses the same simplifying principle, but refers to it as his company's mantra:

> We have our core values, but we also have something that is more like a constitution—we call it our mantra. We filter through it every day, every second of every day. It's taken me, by the way, six years to get this right. So, it was not easy. And I'm a person that does put time into this and loves thinking about this stuff....Our mantra is to *Do good things with good people*....So, we all take the mantra very, very seriously. If anybody just says at any time, "I just don't think they're good people," or, "We can't do good things with them," we're done. It makes it super simple in that regard. We have that high degree of trust with one another, that there's no doubt we can discuss and we can challenge it.

Though it's not always easy to distill a company's overriding principle down to one phrase or sentence, doing so can provide a powerful indicator of a company's core value. This is why taking the time to contemplate one's mission is a valuable use of time. Kitsa Antonopoulos, a Culture Czar client and the founder of Lumiere Children's Therapy, adds this encouragement based on her culture-building experience: "Businesspeople need to give themselves permission to do mental tasks, because we don't think that's work. Carve out the time you need on your calendar. Think things over at your desk or go on a walk—just be sure to carve out the time."

Kitsa knows the value of applied thought. When she tapped me to strengthen Lumiere's culture, she had been thinking about the issues for years. She had not been procrastinating or unwilling to get into core values, but for some time, she felt the exercise was premature—that the company didn't yet have enough history to distill the substance of its purpose. She was right; there needs to be some *doing* before defining of values to ensure there is a legacy from which to build and develop a culture. Although you could draft core values early in the inception of a business, it's always good to keep them fluid in the early stages.

Having recently been through a rebranding, Kitsa was excited to take her new image a step further to reflect her core values—whatever those were. She also knew she wanted to implement a business operating system and a more culture-centric hiring procedure, two things that are also part of the Culture Czars program. (You'll see how to use those tools in concert with your CoreVals in Part Three.) We started out by brainstorming what already existed in her maturing company. We went looking for their core values.

Sometimes we are so close to daily operations that we don't notice the little things that define our culture. As the poet Robert Burns put it: "O, would some power the gift to give us, / to see ourselves as others see us." That's where I come in. I was able to observe Kitsa and her staff, and it was much easier for me—an objective outsider and Culture Czar—to see how they stood out from other organizations and what values were uniquely theirs. Kitsa had already done some groundwork by sitting with her leadership team and brainstorming on the topic. This gave us a starting point from which to build.

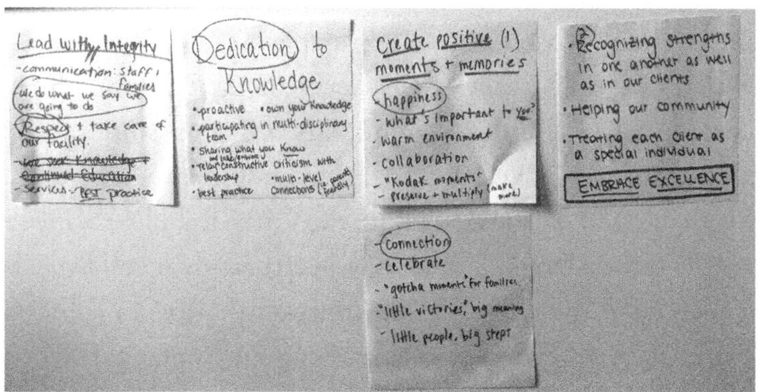

Early notes from Lumiere Children's Therapy initial brainstorming session.

My job was to guide their discovery toward the goal. I helped Kitsa by sitting quietly in her office, observing what went on around me and taking copious notes. The work and clinical spaces at Lumiere are intentionally bright and homey. Because it is a children's therapy practice, the setting is meant to feel welcoming and safe. The therapy starts when you walk in the door. I watched kids run around the living room that serves as a waiting area and pull toys out of the chest and onto the rug. I listened to what the kids and parents were saying, what the staff was saying, and what the whole vibe was saying. In particular, I paid attention to the values displayed by her best employees—the company rock stars, the ones who achieved the most and inspired others. I also observed Kitsa interacting with her team, and I listened to the words she used and the way she used them. I noticed how she would say "you've got this," and "believe it's possible" to scared parents who had just received the diagnosis that their child was autistic. How marvelous when I heard the staff repeating Kitsa's phrases to a child in therapy, "You've got this!"

These sentiments are part of the DNA at Lumiere Children's Therapy. Months or years later, when a child graduates with social skills that parents never thought possible, they become part of Lumiere's community of success stories. They are part of the culture. Those parents now *believe it's possible* for their child to live a fulfilling life. They feel like *they have got this*—the strength and tools to overcome their child's challenges. I call these tag lines descriptive behaviors or subtexts that explain the CoreVals. By observing and listening, I helped Kitsa move beyond rudimentary expressions of her personal values to capture what applied to her company's values.

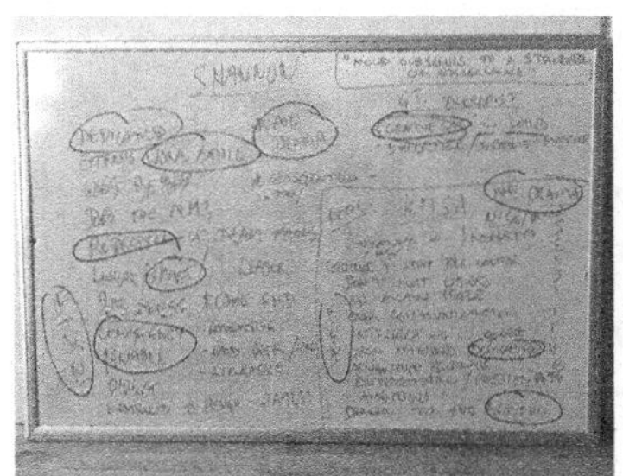

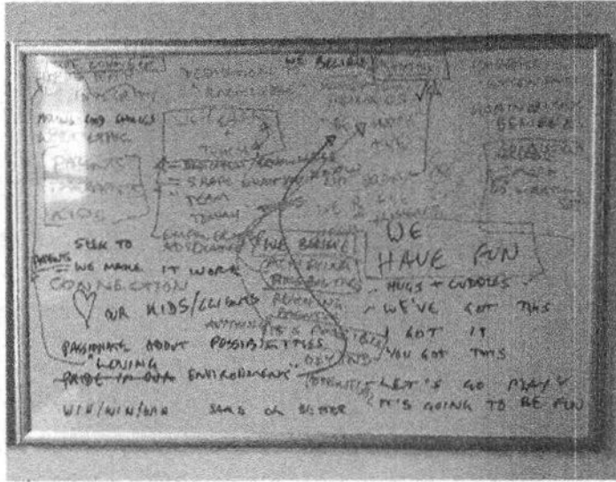

As seen here in Lumiere's early brainstorming sessions, this phase of establishing CoreVals can be messy and chaotic. It's all part of the creative process to get from personal values to a company's values.

We reconvened the leadership team to search more deeply for verbal resonance and to tap into what felt right. We went over my notes looking for repetitive words and themes. Next, on a white board, we put themes into categories. We had one for family goals, one for educational hopes and dreams, and we kept going until four clear values coalesced. We got them by asking hard questions and making lots of observations—about what makes Kitsa tick, why she formed the practice, where she thought Lumiere was going, and how her team operated. This gave us the real purpose of the company—and the values her people would have to act upon to fulfill it. Lumiere's CoreVals were: *Believe, Connect, Teach & Learn,* and *Have Fun.*

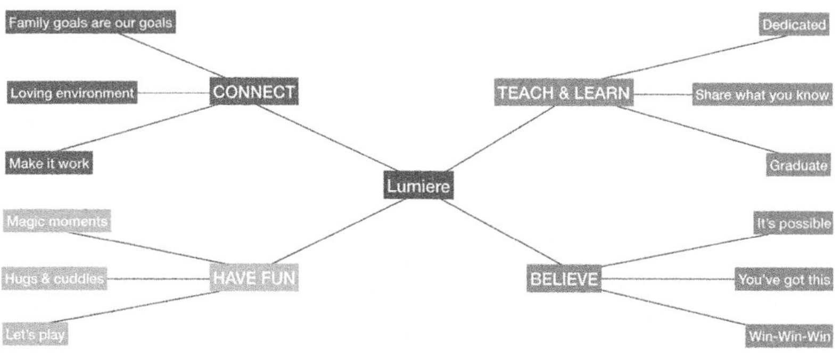

After several brainstorming sessions, Lumiere's CoreVals start to take shape into four distinct areas: *Believe, Connect, Teach & Learn,* and *Have Fun.*

Beautiful stuff, but what does it mean? Even those stellar bits of clarity are not enough to hinge a culture on. I'll show you how to open up the sentiments behind your CoreVals—and the happy result of Kitsa's and Lumiere's soul searching—in Chapter 3. After years of thought, a rebrand in the right direction, and immersion in discovery, Kitsa was well on her way to becoming a Culture Czar. This type of success is not always guaranteed. Focus and sincerity are critical. For now, let's step back and take a look at what happens when you don't do it right.

When Your Culture Train Goes Off Track

Is having no stated values worse than having insufficient ones? Yes. As I mentioned, I learned this painful lesson at my first job out of business school. At that company, there was no set direction of any kind, not even concrete goals. We employees didn't know what we were supposed to be doing as an organization, where we were headed, or how we should function together. This lack of standard made it easy for the owner to arbitrarily criticize and blindside us. Those who risked the least and did nothing to attract notice survived in such an environment that lacked all sense of teamwork or cooperation. I vowed that any company I led would not suffer that same fate.

You may think you're dedicated, but if you are not living, breathing, and talking about those values—keeping them alive—then the culture doesn't thrive and your organization's performance doesn't drive to its full potential.

We've already noted the worst mistake in cultivating a sincere culture is when the CEO and other management leaders are not committed to the CoreVals they have prescribed for everyone else. You may think you're dedicated, but if you are not living, breathing, and talking about those values—keeping them alive—then the culture doesn't thrive and your organization's performance doesn't drive to its full potential. As Mike Petsalis, fellow Culture Czar and CEO of Vircom, shared with me, "There's no on/off switch for culture, it's always on, which means everything you say, everything you do, has to be according to your values and culture. Doing that actually makes it easier to make tough decisions. You just go back to your culture and values."

During your private brainstorming sessions, make a pact with yourself: commit to everyday culture reminders for a healthy period of time. See if you can get to the point where your seventeen-year-old daughter—or your best friend, a supplier, a customer—can repeat the values that you model. If they can do it, then your employees probably can too, and that's a milestone to aim for. Part of putting your intentions into words is making those terms memorable. You may have a string of heartfelt words that push your business forward, however, if no one can recall them, then you are back to an overlooked poster on a wall. And there they stay.

For instance, here is a list of Wells Fargo Bank's stated values:

1. *People as a competitive advantage*
2. *Ethics*
3. *What's right for customers*
4. *Diversity and inclusion*
5. *Leadership*

Easy enough to memorize, but what do they mean? Well, here's the official explanation of the third value:

> We value what's right for our customers in everything we do. We're proud to compete in an industry that's central to the growth of our local, national, and global economies—an industry where doing what's right for customers and communities enables us to make a reasonable profit at the same time. Our customers are our friends. We treat them as our guests. We want them to be successful. We want them to feel as if they're part of Wells Fargo—that we're their company. We want to be approachable and caring, exceed their expectations, and invest in relationships that last a lifetime.[7]

---

7 John G. Stumpf. "The Vision & Values of Wells Fargo." Accessed January 28, 2019. http://www.damicofcg.com/files/74720/Vision%20%26%20Values.pdf.

The Wells Fargo team goes on to explain each value with lengthy paragraphs of more great language, a worthy and needed task that we will get into in the next chapter. However, can the average person remember it? As Dr. Horn's Stanford research asserted, stated values that are not internalized cannot be acted upon. You must live them reflexively in order to genuinely radiate them. That's what you want your people to do: radiate the company's driving forces. That's what forms an identity. That's what customers respond to.

These values are the new and improved version following the bank's fall from grace. Faulty CoreVals may be behind what happened to Wells Fargo: customer exploitation, scandal, and the biggest fine in history. Wells Fargo had glowing CoreVals but blatantly ignored them. They were there in lip service only. *What's right for customers* was a stated value yet they consistently took advantage of millions of customers.

As you get cozy with your CoreVals, walk around and take a look at how your employees do their jobs. What is it that *already* motivates them? These are the nuggets you're searching for. It's great to have ideals and aspirations, but these are not at the core of your organization. As you put your values into words, keep in mind the here and now. Consider the words you have chosen and look objectively at your team and work environment. Then ask yourself, *Do the words feel real? Do they feel too lofty, or do they adequately portray me and my company/organization?*

Perhaps the saddest mistake you can make is to churn out four or five values and call it a day. I have often been called to consult with organizations that settled on a handful of CoreVals, scribbled them on a piece of paper, and stuck them in a desk. They may have told some folks and even emailed them to the rest of the company, but that didn't mean they read them—understood them, memorized them, much less acted on them. This is an incomplete exercise that does nobody any good. It's also part of the reason that the Culture Czar program and the name of the podcast series is *From Core Values to Valued Culture*. It's not enough to simply *have* them, it's what you *do* with them.

Learn from these mistakes so you don't make your own. As you start the first workbook exercise, do it with the intention of following through, knowing that each exercise builds on the previous one. Don't just rattle off the first terms that come to mind. Allow yourself to dive deeply into your own psyche, your company history, and the real "why" of what you do. Allow yourself to reflect and to discover what is already there.

Thoughts from a Culture Czar

"*Having been through four business ventures, I don't think I will ever again start a business without spending a healthy amount of time starting to understand what the business stands for as a brand and backing that down into the core values, because I spent so much time cleaning up mistakes. Suddenly you have a manager who's been with you for four years and now you go through and set the core values and look at them in a meeting thinking 'How the hell is this person here?' It's easy when you can compare them against core values. But in my experience if you don't do it as soon as you can, the cleanup is harder than the implementation.*"

–BRIAN WASPI, CEO CLEAR WATER OUTDOOR

EXERCISE 1: DISCOVER

Before beginning your first brainstorming session, take *The Culture Fix* Checkup found at www.cultureczars.com/the-culture-fix-book. Your results will serve as a baseline to track while you're navigating the Culture Czar process. You will revisit this survey at the end of your 9 Deeds.

The Culture Fix Checkup Results:

Before Score:____________

Comments/Recommendations/Thoughts:

____

____

____

If you prefer to write in a separate workbook that has more room to scribe, visit www.cultureczars.com for a free download of the companion workbook

It's time to explore. Set out to brainstorm, not to set values in stone. Don't hurry. Let your ideas bubble up. Keep in mind that three or four (up to six) CoreVals are a good quantity to learn and embrace fully, while providing enough substance upon which to hang your company's shingle.

In the spaces below, begin to list your organization's philosophies and the stories that make up your history. Jot down unique lingo, inside jokes, phrases that you commonly use or hear—anything related to the substance of your team and your work. Additionally, name your best employees. Now or later, expand on these lists on paper, in a Word doc or, best of all, on a whiteboard with some members of your team. The goal is to create an abundant background from which to select your cultural definition. Keep in mind that the workbook exercises build on each other and that these philosophies will be returned to and expanded upon throughout the workbook.

COMPANY PHILOSOPHIES

____

____

____

____

BUSINESS STORIES

____

____

____

____

UNIQUE LINGO, JOKES, PHRASES

BEST EMPLOYEES

CHAPTER 2

Discern

By stately tower, or palace fair,
Or ruins pendent in the air,
Bold stems of heroes, here and there,
I could discern;
Some seemed to muse, some seemed to dare
With feature stern.

—ROBERT BURNS, THE VISION

CONGRATULATIONS! YOU'VE NOW GOT the raw material you need to get to the heart of your company's motives, purpose, and directional compass. Consider this chapter and its workbook exercise as integral parts of a treasure hunt. You'll be turning over rocks, looking for glimmers of gold and precious stones. This week, you'll continue your private introspection, extrapolating from your answers to Workbook Exercise 1 that put your values, and those of your top staff, into words. You can think about where they intersect or diverge. You can decide whether to compromise, to pull others toward your way of thinking, or to lean toward theirs. You'll find this part of the process enlightening and empowering. It will show you what you have in common with your managers and employees. It will point out the sort of characteristics that forward your agenda. Most importantly, it will hint at what you *don't*

want—what you don't stand for, what does not move the company further along in its purpose and toward its goals.

In Week 2, it's time to identify your innate Culture Czars. As you bring up your new mission over lunch or in communications, pay close attention to the responses. When you see the light come into someone's eyes or you receive effusive, enthusiastic emails supporting your quest, you'll know you've found another czar. You'll take your strongest czars as your confidantes as you deliberately discern your CoreVal priorities and the language that best expresses them. Your Culture Czars will often self-identify by volunteering or showing the most exuberance during the discovery process. It's best to embrace their contributions so that all levels of the company are represented and not simply the leadership. At egalitarian companies like Ink Factory, the owners of the company turned over the task of leading the descriptive behaviors to their Culture Czars completely.

The worst mistake you can make here is not to go deep enough in your self-inquiry, disallowing yourself to share your honest intentions with your team. Authentic culture begins with personal clarity at the top. You don't expect someone else to tell you what is most important to you. The first insights must come from you, the business leader. Core values are certainly your values as well as those of your team and those naturally developed over time within the organization. They're not "out there somewhere;" they're inside you and your organization. You need only discover and reveal them. Every great boss learns: CoreVals must be a part of you, and you must own them more than anybody.

Every great boss learns: CoreVals must be a part of you, and you must own them more than anybody.

Core Values—So Much More Than Just Words

In his book, *Drive: The Surprising Truth About What Motivates Us*, author Daniel Pink captured succinctly what people need in order to feel fulfilled and happy in their work: "Human beings have an innate inner drive to be autonomous, self-determined, and connected to one another. And when that drive is liberated, people achieve more and live richer lives."[8] To this list of employee needs, Daniel Coyle, author of *The Culture Code*, adds safety: "Safety is not mere emotional weather but rather the foundation on which strong culture is built."[9] CoreVals that address and enable these emotional satisfiers help to create healthy environments. Just as laws can protect us, a written code of conduct increases our sense of empowerment, belonging, and safety within the group.

When I started consulting with David Nance, CEO of SABRE Security Equipment Corporation, he had a complicated situation that only cultural improvement could solve. SABRE is the global leader in the manufacture of pepper spray and other safety products for personal and law-enforcement use. The company, founded by Larry Nance in 1975, has been in business for more than forty years, and the family's second generation has been at the helm for some time. Although the enterprise had a long and successful history when I was brought in, it also had some baggage, as all companies do. Morale in the factory and warehouse was low. No matter how solid SABRE's market standing was, sooner or later the drag on productivity was going to take its toll.

---

8 Daniel Pink, *Drive: The Surprising Truth About What Motivates Us* (New York: Penguin Press, 2009), 71.

9 Daniel Coyle, *The Culture Code: The Secrets of Highly Successful Groups* (New York: Random House, 2018), 6.

The emotional needs were not readily met at SABRE, yet there was no reason they couldn't be. The company's size made delegating tasks and decisions to key individuals possible. Those people could then take the initiative to provide other employees with the opportunity to develop some autonomy in their own work. While many lower-level jobs were repetitive or limiting, there was still room to let people work in ways that were most efficient for them, as well as to master what needed to be done to meet objectives and purpose. Pepper spray, home security products, and safety techniques keep people alive and well. Producing it was commendable and should be satisfying.

In such a setting, people *should* feel safe. The greatest signs that an individual feels safe is laughter and frivolity. There weren't enough of these signs at SABRE. The problem was not that executives and employees could not or would not be satisfied. It was that the values by which they could have been working were not solidified or clearly defined. The salient elements of their CoreVals hadn't been deliberately discerned, so they could not be consciously communicated. The CEO made a start and had written some thoughts down, but he knew he had to go further. CoreVals had been circulated but not promoted within the company, nor had they been shared with the broader SABRE community of distributors, customers, and end users. This corporation's situation is quite common and demonstrates how vital it is to bring culture alive and make it thrive so you can drive your people and business toward their full potential.

There were mitigating factors for SABRE, too. The organization was split between two locales, with sales and administrative headquarters in Chicago and the factory and warehouse in St. Louis. The top executive posts were held by family members, who brought some history with them. These conditions influenced the unity of the staff, the flow of communications, and the ability to work as a concerted team.

To make sure I had the full perspective when I began consulting with them, I received input from a large number of the staff through a survey. Next, I interviewed employees looking for common themes, stories, and traits that might illuminate the company's innate CoreVals. This process also allowed me to distinguish who among SABRE was already a Culture Czar and could help the team toward a valued culture.

While we did address the specifics, we went back to the drawing board to do it. In David's case, the rich legacy of stories associated with SABRE's founder and its customers pointed the way to the enduring core values *that were already there.* They simply needed to be discovered, discerned, and developed. In SABRE's case, they emerged from the company's forty storied years of growth under family leadership. It was time to tell those stories.

What Makes Your Company Unique?

In my consultation, I asked SABRE leadership for testimonials and the specifics behind them. Within these, I found three compelling themes:

Humble Beginnings. David's father, Larry Nance, started SABRE with less than three hundred dollars that he won in a national sales contest. His home became his home office; his wife, Jane, became his business partner. They began selling a tear gas formulation, and ten years later, moved into pepper spray research and product development. Larry first sold his merchandise to sporting goods stores, driving as far as his gas money would take him. His vision propelled the start-up to global success, with a formula that ranks as the number-one pepper spray used for protection by police and consumers in more than forty countries. This company has mastered its product.

Heroes. The people who use SABRE products and training programs have their own tales to tell. One customer in a park was able to repel an attacker and escape harm. A college student used her SABRE pepper spray to prevent a rape. A police officer avoided the need for lethal force by deploying his spray canister and apprehending the disabled perpetrator. Not only do customers appreciate the quality and convenience of these potent deterrents, but employees of the company can take pride in making something that literally saves lives.

Partners. SABRE products are especially valuable to scores of law enforcement officers and some of society's most vulnerable members. The company pairs with organizations that protect women at risk for sexual assault, both domestically and in developing countries. Survivors of assault find peace of mind in being armed with protective spray and trained in self-defense. The company donates funds and resources to support these groups that most need their products.

From these themes, David's team and I unearthed the main core values that keep the company running and relevant.

SABRE's Main Core Values:
Proud & Passionate
Empowered
Prepared & Engaged
Go the Extra Mile

These were concrete emotions and conditions to which staff members could relate—once they understood clearly what they stood for. I'll show you how to get to that greater level of precision in Chapter 3, and you'll learn about the positive outcome of SABRE's cultural revolution later in the book. For now, however, let's take one more look at these CoreVals and how they relate to the work experience.

1. *Proud and passionate.* If you're part of the factory or warehouse staff, you need a reason to get out of bed in the morning beyond your hourly pay. SABRE's stories and their business model clearly exemplified what people could be proud of:

- The founder's dedication, vision, and persistence
- The family-owned company
- The long company history and loyalty to its community
- Products made in America and tested onsite
- Being the global market leader
- Protection of people's health and safety

Pride in these factors, plus the company's special support of women's health and safety, made those who worked there passionate about what they did—at that point, they just didn't know it yet. In my opinion, three words—*proud and passionate*—are not enough to reveal their scope. This is why we need the subtexts, or descriptive behaviors, to explain what SABRE's people mean by those words. The context lends specificity to the value. You'll read the full descriptions later, but the two that we came up with for this value were:

- We are proud of our mission to save and our global leading brands.
- We are passionate about our heroes, our team, and our customers.

With these explainers, SABRE's products moved from lowly aerosol cans propelling pepper spray to life-savers that turned customers into "heroes." Now *that's* changing a perspective and the way people feel about their work.

2. *Empowered.* This value could be shared by employees, customers, and senior management alike, as I found out. Clearly, being armed with an effective repellant against attackers, home invaders, and even aggressive animals is empowering, no matter who you are. Men, women, children, police officers, prison guards, and consumers of all stripes gain power from the pepper.

I wanted to give everyone a reason to carry forth SABRE's values. Internally, empowerment meant more freedom to perform tasks as workers saw fit. This entailed building trust across management and staff. Executives and managers felt empowered to delegate, trusting that their goals would be pursued in line with the company's best interests. Among the sibling administrative team, building culture from common values created another kind of empowerment—it leveled the playing field so that everybody's ideas and concerns were received with open minds, rather than by job title or birth order.

3. *Prepared and engaged.* This value relates to both work ethic and the result of that work. Being ready to hop on an eagerly awaited order serves customers who may be in dire need. Doing the job right at the factory, test site, and warehouse gives consumers the tools they need to be prepared and engaged—to support a 360-degree awareness of their environments while increasing personal security. This CoreVal tells workers what they need to do, which is be ready and willing to do what it takes in their roles. It also gives a nod to their larger purpose in the company—to prepare and engage others in their own safety.

4. *Go the extra mile.* This CoreVal also relates to what the company expects of workers and what it gives to its customers. When sales and production need to be high, staff must jump in the boat and row together. In a medium-sized, family-owned company, staying ahead of the competition by pleasing customers is crucial. Satisfying those customers so they can go beyond their comfort zones in an emergency—perhaps going the extra mile to protect a loved one or stranger—is the result of their efforts.

What corporations consistently operate in line with their stated values? Or, to put it better, which companies do consumers perceive as doing so? Let's go with a leader, Apple

Inc. Apple's founder, Steve Jobs, knew the value of having CoreVals and sharing them with the public. He once said, "It's a complicated and noisy world, and we're not going to get a chance to get people to remember much about us. No company is. We have to be really clear about what we want them to know about us."[10] In another interview, he explained how Apple's core values remained their North Star as they weathered conflicts that came with a growing company:

> [T]he worst thing that could possibly happen as we get big and we get a little more influence in the world, is if we change our core values and start letting it slide. I can't do that. I'd rather quit....We're certainly a little more experienced, we're certainly more beat up, but the core values are the same. And we come into work wanting to do the same thing today as we did five or ten years ago which is build the best products for people....That's what keeps me going. And it's what kept me going five years ago. It's what kept me going ten years ago when the doors were almost closed, and it's what'll keep me going five years from now, whatever happens.[11]

As Jobs explained, core values are constant. The market might change, the culture might change, but the core values remain the same. They create order out of chaos. The company's current CEO, Tim Cook, reiterated the following core values statement:

---

10 *Steve Jobs Marketing Strategy,* YouTube video, 6:58, posted by "Inspiring Videos," February 28, 2015, https://www.youtube.com/watch?v=mMBQwAe45jc.

11 *Steve Jobs talks About Core Values at D8 2010,* YouTube video, 2:28, posted by "SteveNote," January 5, 2012, https://www.youtube.com/watch?v=5m-KxekNhMqY&feature=youtu.be.

- We believe that we're on the face of the Earth to make great products.
- We believe in the simple, not the complex.
- We believe that we need to own and control the primary technologies behind the products we make.
- We participate only in markets where we can make a significant contribution.
- We believe in saying no to thousands of projects so that we can really focus on the few that are truly important and meaningful to us.
- We believe in deep collaboration and cross-pollination of our groups, which allow us to innovate in a way that others cannot.
- We don't settle for anything less than excellence in every group in the company, and we have the self-honesty to admit when we're wrong and the courage to change.[12]

I had the privilege of working closely with Apple at Lextech, my mobile app development business, and I witnessed firsthand how they always acted in concert with their stated values. They were consistently clear about what they would do and more importantly what they would not do. Let's look at two of those "values" more closely. These sentiments are striking in their capacity *to be supported* by the company's representatives. "We believe in saying no to thousands of

12 Adam Lashinsky, "The Cook Doctrine at Apple," *Fortune,* January 22, 2009, http://fortune.com/2009/01/22/the-cook-doctrine-at-apple/.

projects so that we can really focus on the few that are truly important and meaningful to us." Admitting that a focus on priorities entails weeding out certain prospects is sincere and easily lived up to.

The final "value" on the list is not an easily attainable goal, but the description acknowledges that and points to what will happen if at first the company fails in that pursuit—it will try again, and try something different until it does succeed.

In establishing your company's or organization's core values, ask yourself how well you follow them on a daily basis. Be honest. No one expects you to "do the right thing" all of the time. What about when the unexpected happens, when meetings get cancelled and culture takes a back seat? It's easy for leaders to lose sight of things when we find ourselves in the weeds. That happens in any business.

If you know you are particularly susceptible, take steps to avoid or alleviate becoming overwhelmed. Delegate. Be more strict in scheduling your time. Resolve not to let anything interfere with meeting your goals, which now include keeping CoreVals and culture among your priorities. If you do find yourself in the weeds, don't be afraid to admit it and accept your own shortcomings. I, myself, have admitted right in my company blog, "A busy spell at work has caused me to pause in writing this blog, and it feels like I might not have given our culture the priority it deserves. This is a danger we can all succumb to, and I of all people, need to keep [core values] front and center in order to maintain them." If you are an effective CEO, founder, owner, or other type of company leader, you already know how to capitalize on your strengths. The question now is, how will you work on your weaknesses?

CoreVals show how a company can extend beyond the employees to a company's customers, and how leaders can lead a culture that extends well beyond the four walls of an organization. As Dee Robinson, founder and president of Robinson Hill, shared with me during an interview for the Culture Czar podcast, creating a work culture has the capability to change the lives of the people who engage with it:

> I love the fact that people will walk out of work thinking, *I have better opportunities to change the trajectory of my life at home with family.* These are values that I know can carry them in this job or any other job and help lead to continued success. That's what I want for all our people. I want them to lead successful lives, both personally and professionally. What we do in our lives, hopefully, we'll do in our jobs.

In addition to changing the world within a business, asking people to be more engaged with their values can change the way they conduct themselves in all areas of life. The ripple effect of creating an intentional company culture has the potential to change the lives of individuals, their families, their communities, and their worlds.

At Lumiere Children's Therapy, their CoreVals poster displays their four core values. It also illuminates how team members can use their thoughts and behaviors to further illuminate each value. In this way, core values are not merely words on a poster; they're thoughts and actions that have the capacity to change the lives of all they touch.

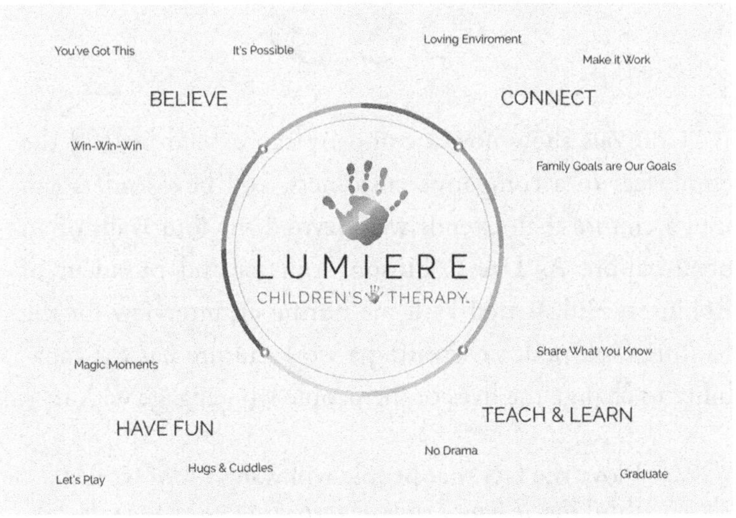

Lumiere Children's Therapy CoreVals Poster

To review in more detail, visit www.cultureczars.com

You can see how just a few well-turned words and phrases can speak volumes more than their dictionary definitions. Now that you know how and why to refine your stories, themes, and company lingo, you can get one step closer to putting those core values on the wall and into people's hearts and minds. Complete the next workbook exercise, and you'll be ready to do that.

Thoughts from a Culture Czar

> *Culture [is] simple, but it's incredibly complicated to pull off.…I think it's a ship without the rudder without the core values.…The way I simplify it in my head is 'vibe.' What is the vibe? I mean, you can feel it when it's right. And I believe you can feel it when it's wrong. So if you have the right culture, or the wrong culture even, you can feel it through the vibe.*
>
> – DAN HEUERTZ, THE PREFERRED GROUP

EXERCISE 2: DISCERN

Look back on what you wrote in Exercise 1 and use it to complete Task A, below. Then, invite your best Culture Czars to help you delve more deeply to produce a shortlist of terminology for your CoreVals in Task B. A heads-up: you may need to return to Week 2 from time to time to get your thoughts and your words just right and to align your Core-Vals with your current status in the workplace, marketplace, and world. Throughout the process, continue to ask yourself if your words feel real. This could be the most important task in your organization's life.

A. Review the language associated with your company and its stories in Exercise 1. Imagine and project which values you think your best employees exhibit. Then write down your own personal values and the values that best represent how your company fulfills its purpose.

BEST EMPLOYEE VALUES

____

____

____

____

OWNER/FOUNDER/CEO's VALUES

____

____

____

____

____

____

B. Get your team together and consider what you have chosen as CoreVal priorities. Circle the top five to eight words or phrases from Task A above. Collaborate with the team and add some descriptions of what they think the values mean in the context of your organization.

TOP FIVE TO EIGHT WORDS/PHRASES

____

____

ADD MEANING AND CONTEXT TO THOSE TERMS

CHAPTER 3

Describe

Through many a wild, romantic grove,
Near many a hermit-fancied cove
(Fitting haunts for friendship or for love
In musing mood),
An aged Judge, I saw him rove,
Dispensing good.

—ROBERT BURNS, THE VISION

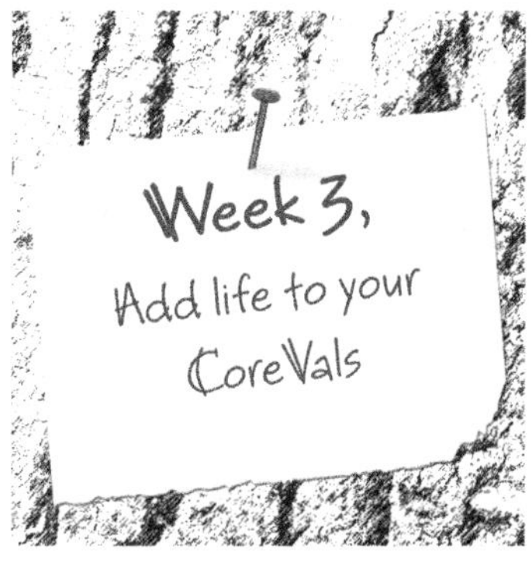

PART ONE OF THIS cultural journey is all about putting thoughts, feelings, and beliefs into words. That is not an easy task! Perhaps that's because we don't practice doing it enough. We seldom express ourselves effectively in conversation. We rely on context, tone of voice, and assumptions about the receiver's ability to understand our intended meaning before we say it. In his book, *Find Your Why,* Simon Sinek uses the example of being in love to demonstrate how difficult it is to put nebulous concepts into words: "There's just one problem with feelings. They can be tremendously difficult to express in words. That's the reason we so often resort to metaphors and analogies."[13] In trying to describe the object of our devotion, for example, we dance around the topic, lighting

13 Simon Sinek, *Find Your Why: A Practical Guide to Discovering Purpose for You or Your Team* (New York: Penguin Press, 2017), 16.

on characteristics that we love about a person, like being funny or smart. Or we use euphemisms that get close, "She completes me." Being unable to express *why* we love someone is not a conscious failure. As Sinek notes, our brains are segmented. The portion that registers emotion does not "speak" with the portion that forms language.

Does that stop us from trying to say what we mean? No. And in the context of building culture, it only means that we must work harder at it. Our first version of CoreVals at Lextech totaled 389 words. The words were there, but we needed something short and sweet that people could remember, yet it had to be rich with meaning. That's when the true sentiments come into stark relief. When you chip away at the stone, you find the masterpiece inside. In our case, we unearthed five very apt core values. In order to make them more fun and more compelling, we worked with our in-house designers to give them superhero personas that would appeal to a group of mostly technical folks who adored science fiction and comic books. Like *The Avengers* or *Fantastic Four*, our superheroes soon became known to our group as *The Core*. We wanted them to be accessible and crystal-clear to everyone else, too. That's where further description came in.

How to Say What Your Core Values Mean

When we got to the Describe phase of Lextech's CoreVals development, we were still feeling our way. Having summarized and superhero-ized our core values, we wanted to add some descriptions that would let us know when we were living them. We asked ourselves, *How would someone new to the team know what we meant when we challenged each other to "grow" or "deliver success?"*

We hit the white board and wrote down some descriptive behaviors that supported the values. From there, we winnowed it all down to just the information that an uninformed reader would need to understand our intentions. We added subheadings that described what lay at the root of our values.

Captain Client

Clients come first. We added: Client→Team→Self. We observed that right from the start, we had always cared about the client and innately wanted to do great work for them. If it was 5 p.m. on a Friday and we hadn't delivered on an end-of-week promise, none of us was going to abandon the client or the team. Identifying our action helped us decipher our descriptive behavior or attribute for this value.

We build lasting relationships. We were talking about basing our priorities on good customer relations, which we believed would serve our company best in the long-term. It left no wiggle room when making decisions that involved clients.

The early version of Captain Client was born after numerous brainstorming sessions on what descriptive behaviors supported our core value *Clients come first*.

The final version of Captain Client.

Passionista

Exude passion and energy. We were a team that was energetic and excitable about our work. We started early, competed to be the one at the white board, and were eager to share our ideas and try something new. We knew we wanted to maintain this feeling, so we captured it.

We are confident and can-do. We believed we could solve just about any problem, and we liked to say "yes." In fact, we adopted the phrase "yes and," and liked to correct each other if we said "yes but."

We live the technology, and it excites us. This captured our attitude towards the possibilities and beliefs that we shared regarding mobile technology and the power of apps.

The final version of Passionista.

Danny Deliver

Deliver success takes some integrity. Did we have it?

We care and we do what we say. We did. But how did we know we could keep our promises?

We follow process so that success repeats. By doing what worked every time, we couldn't go wrong.

The final version of Danny Deliver.

Tea and Wok

Work as a team is more easily said than done. We needed to prove our commitment to teamwork with all members. How did we do that?

We respect and help others. This showed that we appreciated individuals' gifts and were ready to support each other. But how did we make the most of the team's efforts?

The final version of Tea & Wok.

We listen and provide feedback. We could all be better at listening, and we all want to be heard. This statement reminded us to be intentional about it and notice when someone wasn't doing it. We believed in this value for the sake of team health.

Grow'n

Grow could just mean expanding the company in size and market share, yet to us it meant more.

We embrace change and invest in our future. That would help the company grow, too. But what about us?

We teach and encourage learning. We knew growth was about much more than the bottom line.

The early version of Grow'n was born after numerous brainstorming sessions on what descriptive behaviors supported our core value of *Grow*.

The final version of Grow'n.

Note the use of "we" for every Lextech statement above. This not only conveys inclusion and belonging, it suggests a more personal commitment or promise to the group. With this second, more polished round of discernment, our word count dropped from 389 to 91 and became more memorable, engaging, and much more likely to be effective. *Less is more* proved to be true, and it is worth the effort to distill the message.

Now we had core values that implied the company's purpose and that defined what we wanted our process and our work environment to be. Most importantly, it was people-centric. When everyone moved with the flow of these values, Lextech would be a place where people would thrive and be the best that they could be. You could easily argue that there is some overlap with these values and observe that one statement might make another one redundant. In fact, this only strengthens the values as a cohesive whole. You know you have accurately described a *culture* when the values hang together and support each other to create an overall feeling. Remember that we need enough detail in the words or the imagery to leave little room for doubt about what we mean by a certain value.

You'll know when your core values click because they will make life better for everyone in the metaphorical tree house. Getting back to that issue of prioritizing customer happiness, the CoreVal that states, *We build lasting relationships*, acts as guidance in specific situations, even when company leaders are absent. For example, suppose the team was deliberating whether to charge a client more with a pricing decision that would pull revenue into this fiscal year and boost the company's bottom line. In the short-term, that could be great for our company, but it could hurt the client. A supervisor might argue, "Why not go for the profit? That will boost our bonus!" That action would not put the client first and would violate the stated value. It would be easy to shoot down that idea by pointing to the core value, *We build lasting relationships*. There is no argument. Putting the client's needs first and building the long-term relationship would ultimately better serve the company. It is important to have everybody on board with that. Now we have fully actualized images that elucidate our core values and defining behaviors: *The Core*.

The Core brings Lextech's core values and descriptive behaviors to life.

To review in more detail,
visit www.cultureczars.com

How to Connect Viewers with Your Values

When a group is diverse, yet makes the same decision given the same set of circumstances, a certain power is unleashed in the organization. Instilling your core values in each member of the team can do that. Similarly, *We listen and provide feedback* carries some valuable protections for the group. Recall that feeling safe on a team is imperative. Respectful communication is part of that equation. When someone feels like they are not being heard, it's a beautiful thing to be able to cite the need to adhere to this core value, assuring they have the support of the team, the leadership, and the organization as a whole.

At my first company, Waer Systems, we addressed group support under the CoreVal of *Respect* like this:

- We hold our colleagues, partners, and customers in high regard.
- We are open about issues, plans, results, and problems.
- We trust each other and are not shy of conflict-for-good.

This value made life better for all in the company because it provided a platform for difficult conversations. It allowed us to freely give and receive important feedback. What a gift to any team that is plagued by festering issues, such as someone's annoying habit or suffering through hurt feelings. This type of CoreVal effectively gives permission to take someone aside and provide feedback and also ensures it is done respectfully.

WAER Systems
Supply Chain Technologies

Culture, Values and Behaviours

The following values and behaviours define our culture. We believe that we are all equally accountable for our company values:

Integrity
We act legally, ethically, and responsibly
We make decisions in the interest of the long term
We keep our promises

Respect
We hold our colleagues, partners and customers in high regard
We are open about issues, plans, results and problems
We trust each other and are not shy of conflict-for-good

Commitment
We care and we go the extra mile
We are enthusiastic and maintain a positive attitude
We know what we have to do and we get on with it

Technical Excellence
We excel at what we do
We embrace learning, change and new technologies
We design and install good product

Waer Systems CoreVals and descriptive behaviors.

What about our CoreVals at Culture Czars? I will share our CoreVals and other corporate culture assets in the pages that follow. As we are a new and relatively small organization, our CoreVals were developed within the last twelve months. They are firm, but we have intentionally left room for improvement and validation as we mature over the next year. We can say though that they *feel* good to us (which is the first step), and that we are already experiencing the expected benefits.

We discerned the values that were important to us and then articulated them with words from our lingo, like *sawubona.* Using our own stories and verbiage helped us capture the respect we have for our collective culture and the recognition we offer to each individual. We care how everyone is feeling and we make sure everyone is included. The word *sawubona* worked and was easily depicted by a human eye to further the message of "I see you." We had our first value. We ruminated on it and asked ourselves in some quiet contemplation, *Does it feel real?* It did.

Next we discussed timeless traditions and the source of societal and familial values as they related to us. One recurring theme was the importance of doing what we said we would do and simply being *reliable.* Another was the universal experience of working through loss or pain to become a stronger, more evolved human. Regardless of the experiences, we kept showing up, and this led to the value of *stoicism.* How could this be any better represented than by the mighty baobab tree that is such a solid symbol of reliability, yielding its goodness season after season and millennia after millennia? It was also the right value upon which to hang our zest for life, which we deemed *life's love.* Using the baobab tree to symbolize these values felt real to us and unique to the culture we wanted to propagate.

Another value that coalesced during our brainstorming sessions was feeling blessed and lucky to have so much knowledge, talent, and opportunity among us, as well as a desire to freely share and give back. I shared a story with the team of when my father was running a sheep research station in the Andes during my teenage years. He was assigned this fascinating project after his work in Zambia and later earned an OBE from the British government for his achievements in developing a new breed of sheep that thrived in the high elevations. I was on holiday from boarding school in Ireland and had just ridden a mule up to the *fiesta* that my father was hosting for the workers. I noticed that none of the men finished his beer. Every beer bottle on the table had some left in the bottom. Those drinking outside poured the last sips of beer on the ground. I wondered why people who appeared to have so little would waste their drink. Later that day, I asked my father. He explained that it was *abundancia,* meaning "I have enough." They demonstrated this shared value by refusing the last drop. I realized that even though they appeared to have so little, they were content and lived their lives with an attitude of abundance.

The story resonated with the team and it captured our value. When hiring, we wanted to bring in others with the same value. We wanted people who could see endless possibilities and could focus on abundance rather than scarcity. This value was captured by the word *abundancia.* Based on the Bible verse, "My cup runneth over," we depicted it with an image of an overflowing cup.

At Culture Czars, we found our CoreVals and associated imagery to be so self-explanatory that fewer descriptive behavior words were required. A word like *Churchillian,* for example, needs little embellishment because much of this great man's values are summed up in the mention of his name. Most people know what he stood for in terms of leadership, determination, and "never ever ever give up." What applied to our team's character more than anything was inspiration, exuberance, and humor. We are stirred by our mission and motivate others through our work. We are exuberant too and embrace humor. These are the aspects from Churchill that we lift up and honor most in our work together. Because CoreVals tie together and are used in concert with one another, we didn't need to go with fortitude or stoicism because they were already covered by baobab. Churchill and baobab together were covering more of our sacred ground. This felt like it was working and it will for you too when you go through the process.

Baobab, *Sawubona*, *Abundancia,* and *Churchillian*. Did they feel real? Yes, very much so. Once we identified the values, we applied meaningful badges or nick-names to them and created the imagery or icons that supported them. The end result is what we hope you will achieve: captured values that are brought alive, easily communicated and remembered, easily adopted and reinforced.

We now have our own language for our "tree house" and it helps us communicate efficiently, remain on the same page, and make decisions guided by our principles. It is easy to say "let's be sure to delight the client with this delivery" or "what else can we give?" or "do you think we made them feel included enough?"

Since it is often helpful to observe the process of going from core values to a valued culture before embarking on your own, I will continue to share Culture Czars progression. In the chapters that follow you will see how we carried our CoreVals forward into our CoreWorkflow and finally our CoreChart.

CoreVals should be real and existing—not wishful thinking. There are such things as dormant virtues. As you move through culture-building, you will animate your company's most important values. Take the discernment and description tasks seriously until you find and awaken them. Enlivening culture is a process, but once set in motion, it keeps building and evolving in the right direction. One other important element that lends perspective to this process is knowing the company's collective purpose or vision. It is the essential glue that binds coworkers to coworkers as well as the whole team to its leadership. I like to call this the CorePurpose—the overarching company goal and reason for being.

CorePurpose is the *why* and *what* for the business. It tells employees what they are working toward and why. It is motivating and energizing, and somehow comforting. Once spelled out, a company's purpose gives everyone a reason to *be*, to work, and to believe in what they are doing. While CoreVals will help employees in your company love *where* they work, the CorePurpose will help them love *why* they work.

Some employees may get this intrinsically from their work and coworker admiration because they are A-players who are motivated and love what they do. A statement that provides purpose and meaning will help everyone feel this way about their work because they will all understand why it matters. You can see how vital it is to precisely detail your company's values and purpose so they can guide your team's actions. In this way, everyone becomes a leader, and you really are solving C-suite problems at the ground level before they even begin.

Thoughts from a Culture Czar

"*[Culture] is not something that you can rank and put on the back burner to focus on later. It's something that needs to be focused on every single day, but in small increments. You're living the core values and you have a strong, healthy culture—or you don't. We've seen the moods of offices increase and decrease, so just like in a household, everybody could be crabby for awhile, [or] everybody could be in a great mood. We see that going on in offices and we'll do something proactive to be able to create a more positive environment...but it doesn't change the overall culture of the company. Keeping a strong, healthy culture is something that we try to [focus on] every day.*"

—TONY MIRCHANDANI,
CEO OF RTM ENGINEERING CONSULTANTS

EXERCISE 3: DESCRIBE

Break out the markers and hit the white board with your Culture Czars. Let's get to the core of your company's beliefs and words to live by. Put all your ideas into the grinder and keep turning until you're left with bite-sized nuggets of wisdom. You can use the examples in this chapter as guidelines for your finished product.

From the five to eight major values you listed in Exercise 2, choose your priorities. Three or four are ideal, six is the recommended maximum. It has been my experience over countless interviews with employees that they can rarely remember more than four. Beneath those, list the most succinct descriptors from your white board session.

Try to avoid hackneyed and overused values like *respect* and *integrity*, unless you assign them deeper meanings. Then spend some time wordsmithing until you are done. Hopefully, you will have some catch phrases, rhymes, acronyms, or something so unique that you are the only company in the world with that value. As an example, see the results below that Culture Czars attained when we went through our own process.

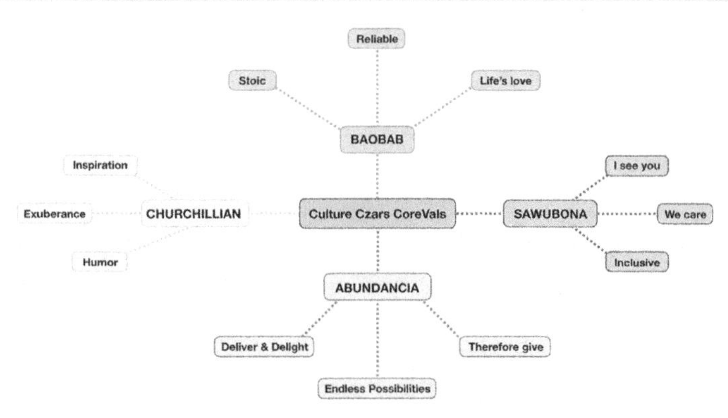

Final Culture Czars CoreVals

 To review in more detail, visit www.cultureczars.com

COREVAL 1

COREVAL 2

COREVAL 3

COREVAL 4

(COREVAL 5)

(COREVAL 6)

PART TWO:
THRIVE

Take Your Core Values to the People (and Beyond)

- ✓ Design
- ✓ Decree
- ✓ Dictate

CHAPTER 4

Design

With deep-struck, reverential awe,
The learned Sire and Son I saw:
To Nature's God, and Nature's law,
They gave their lore;
This, all its source and end to draw,
That, to adore.

—ROBERT BURNS, THE VISION

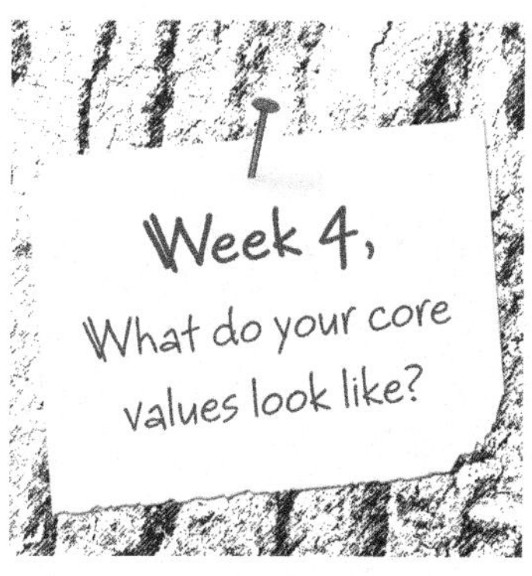

YOUR MISSION IN PART Two of this book is to get some creative input and decide on a theme and style for print materials, meeting agendas, and the core values rollout event itself. It will also help you memorialize your core values so that others will remember them. The suspense and excitement among your leadership team and the passion of your Culture Czars will grow as you plan how to bring your message to the masses. In order for your values, your people, and your company's culture to thrive, you must integrate your newly clarified CoreVals into everyday life in the workplace.

Creating print displays for your core values and their descriptors is a must. Unless CoreVal words are highlighted in some graphic way and hung on the wall, they really don't exist and aren't part of the culture. Simply having them in an email or on the company wiki/intranet is not effective. I like to see CoreVals on posters, pocket cards, and put in front of everybody in creative ways via customized key rings, coffee mugs, or some other everyday item—especially if it is pertinent to your business. Home screen displays for any digital device is probably the single most effective display you could choose as well as laptop stickers. Office posters, or even a mural, will also be effective. Keeping CoreVals hidden suggests the company is not proud enough or serious enough about them. You'll need several print iterations of your descriptive core values, which ideally are part of a multimedia affair. The big reveal should happen at a company-wide gathering. However you connect with your team, your delivery system will be a thoughtfully composed speech that sums up your vision for the company's culture.

The Lextech's CoreVals mural.

The best way to start showcasing your core values is to get your core team together and decide on a theme first. It doesn't have to be fun or funny—let it reflect your organization's style or market niche. If you're a bunch of academics, maybe riffing on titles of the classics will work for you. If you're people-oriented like SABRE, pictures of customers can drive home your sincerity about your values. If you work with children, like the therapists at Lumiere Children's Therapy, small hands or toy trains add meaning to the words on the wall.

Take special care in designing your visual theme because it will get a lot of use. Spinoffs from the all-important poster might include website decor, "flash" cards that you hand out to all employees, or promotional items emblazoned with your CoreVals. One effective theme was devised by the science fiction fans at the email security firm, Vircom.

Get It Done!

- Commits, delivers
- Results-oriented
- No excuses, no bullshit

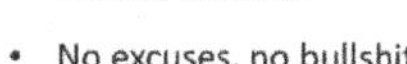

Find a Better Way!

- Always solving and improving
- Overcomes obstacles
- Undaunted by failure

Delight Your Customer!

- Exceeds expectations
- Listens, understands, then acts
- Respects and empathizes

Always keep learning!

- Learns enthusiastically and applies
- Shares, teaches
- Seeks feedback

Vircom's *Star Trek*-themed core values poster.

Here is a visual about values that is instantly recognizable to large segments of the general population. In considering what would illustrate their values, the core team at Vircom realized that four iconic characters from the *Star Trek* television show and films embodied their traits. Captain Kirk, Scotty, Mr. Spock, and Bones fiercely display their values in their roles. These personal and shared values are things everyone can relate to, and they definitely bring their CoreVals alive. Vircom also has its CoreVals displayed prominently on the company website for the world to see. This language is so engrained at Vircom that one entire value theme can be summed up with a simple reference to Scotty and his *Get it Done* ways.

> A common misconception is that core values are for internal consumption only—that they will never be communicated outside the organization. That's a big mistake and a lost opportunity.

Remember that all eyes may be on your display someday. A common misconception is that core values are for internal consumption only—that they will never be communicated outside the organization. That's a big mistake and a lost opportunity. CoreVals can be effective when floated downstream to customers and the general public, and upstream to vendors and colleagues. It helps spread your unique culture to the greater community, aligning your best clients and vendors with your company's mission. When difficult conversations become necessary with clients and vendors, or even your company's attorneys, accountants, and other service people, those discussions are made easier with the use of core values. You have an objective rationale for your actions and can do what has to be done without provoking personal animosity.

If they're already aware of these criteria, so much the better.

Remember you are leading a culture that extends beyond the four walls of the company. Take Vircom's first CoreVal, *Get It Done*. Its descriptive behavior says, "Make commitments and deliver; be results oriented without any excuses." Let's say Vircom was selecting a new vendor or partner. During the interview, they might mention, "We work best with partners that fit our culture and subscribe to our values. Are you ready to be held accountable to our *Get It Done* core value?" If so, when it comes to onboarding, Vircom could ask them to display the company's CoreVals prominently in front of the team that will be working on its account. If and when the vendor has a disruption in service and tries to make excuses for not delivering, Vircom's conversation is a lot easier. They also have a better chance of maintaining a successful relationship and getting service back on track by referencing core values instead of the service level agreement. An appeal to the vendors' best human nature may actually be stronger than a binding legal document. This is just one way CoreVals can extend beyond the corporation and be used to lead a culture, not just a company. The same logic applies downstream of your business too. Have you noticed that your best clients or customers are those that align with your values?

Your organization's CoreVals may not lend themselves to outside themes like superheroes or starship officers. Instead, you can personalize them through the use of the stories associated with your business, as SABRE did with its use of real-life "heroes." The SABRE core team identified employees and customers who represent distinct values—like the Uber driver who does her job with confidence because she is empowered to prevent an attack, or the child safety expert who displays his passion for protection as a trainer for the SABRE Personal Safety Academy.

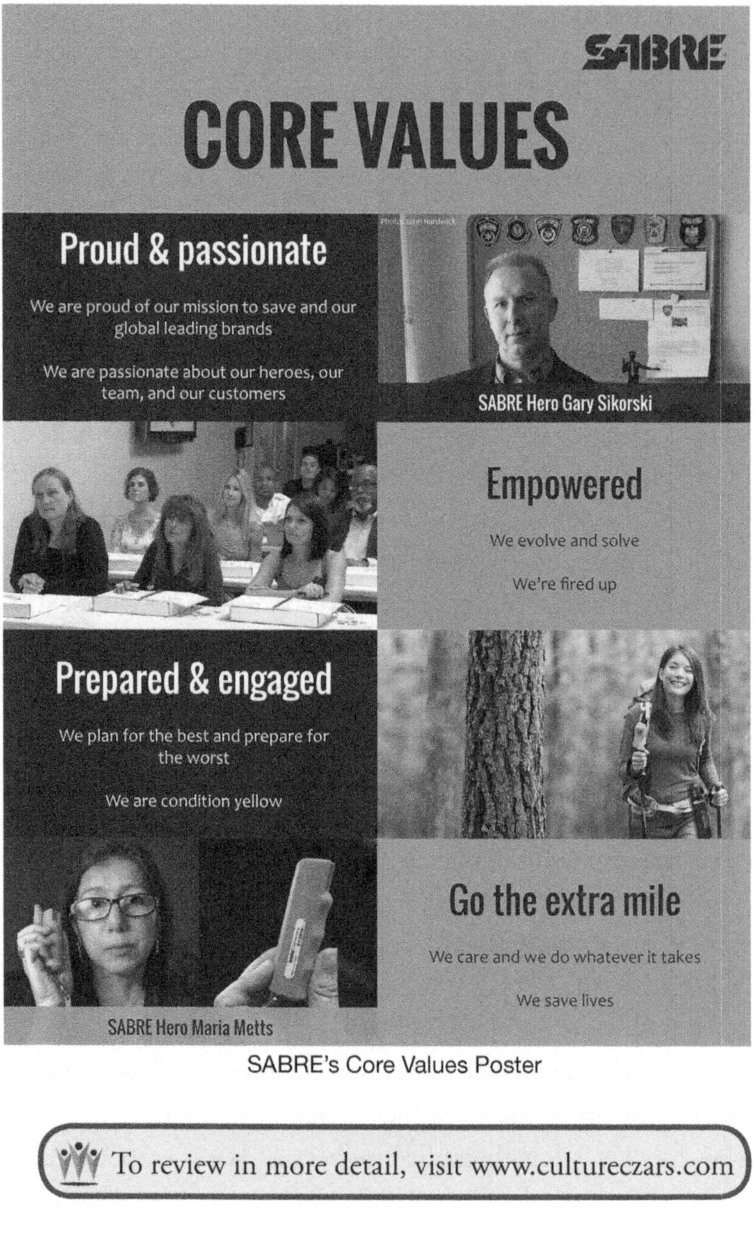

SABRE

CORE VALUES

Proud & passionate

We are proud of our mission to save and our global leading brands

We are passionate about our heroes, our team, and our customers

SABRE Hero Gary Sikorski

Empowered

We evolve and solve

We're fired up

Prepared & engaged

We plan for the best and prepare for the worst

We are condition yellow

Go the extra mile

We care and we do whatever it takes

We save lives

SABRE Hero Maria Metts

SABRE's Core Values Poster

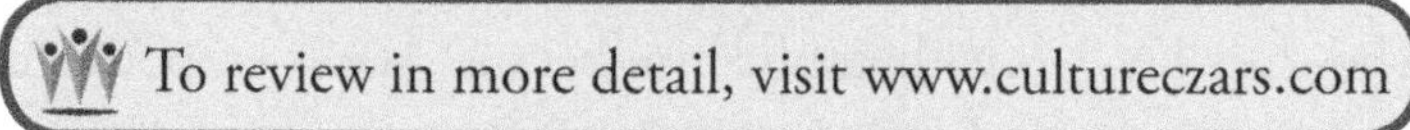

As you go about this creative process, be thinking ahead. How will you use your presentation to keep your CoreVals in the minds of employees daily, weekly, and monthly? We'll get to the functional use of meeting time to remind folks of your company's values and purpose in Chapter 5. Now, I'd like to introduce a key way to get those sentiments off the wall and into your people's psyches via the monthly award.

Off the Wall and into Hearts and Minds

Acknowledging your staff's work is part of good business management. Tying that recognition to your core values is one more way to bring them front and center, and to show how integral they are to daily operations. You can use company lore to illustrate CoreVals, much like using word problems to make arithmetic more germane to students. If you hand out a $5 gift card to your top salesperson once a month, people will just yawn and go back to their desks. If you show your gratitude for demonstrating a value that defines your group, *based on company history that everyone knows,* you've got context. You've got Aha! moments. You are also tapping emotions, making people feel connected and, of course, having fun. Before you know it, you've got people doing their best to be next in line for that prize. We're not just talking about a free coffee at Starbucks. Make it something that people really want and will appreciate. One way to do this is to ask your team what their interests are and what would make them feel special. Show that you've made an effort to make the prize personal to the individual.

Once again, the folks at SABRE handled this task with style. They take nominations from the employees themselves for the coworker who best lives up to one of the company's CoreVals that month. And they do it for every department.

Then, everyone gets together in the warehouse and one member of the leadership team announces the winner of the "228 Award." Stories are told, values are reinforced, and one person from each department goes home with a $250 gift certificate. The sum is rounded up from $228—the amount of money that Larry Nance initially invested to found SABRE in 1975. Do you think any member of SABRE has forgotten about the roots of their business? Not a chance. Where the company came from is an important part of its current identity. It's one of the things in which people take pride. Reminding the staff of this every month keeps that particular value alive. At these gatherings, it is important not to just name the winner, but to tell the story behind the nomination and the CoreVal for which the employee was nominated. To show that culture extends beyond the internal organization, even I was awarded SABRE's Empowered Award for helping the corporation "evolve and solve" its cultural challenges.

PROJECT 228

A monthly $228 bonus recognizing the best employee examples of our core values

In 1975, at the young age of 27, Larry Nance took a major leap of faith and invested his entire savings into starting Security Equipment Corporation. That $228.00 investment along with the hard work of SABRE Team Members has led to over 4 decades of success and SABRE – Security Equipment Corporation becoming the #1 pepper spray sold worldwide. From young students to men in uniform, SABRE has increased the personal safety of tens of millions. Our hard work has also resulted in approximately 14,000 free mammograms to support the fight against breast cancer. There are a number of very impressive milestones and accomplishments to celebrate.

Speaking of celebration, in honor of our founder and the foundation of success and hard work he created for us, we would like to honor one team member each month whose efforts most closely resemble our core values.

Proud & Passionate

- We are proud of our mission to save and our global leading brands
- We are passionate about our heroes, our team, and our customers

Empowered

- We evolve and solve
- We're fired up

Prepared and Engaged

- We plan for the best and prepare for the worst
- We are condition yellow

Go the Extra Mile

- We care and we do whatever it takes
- We save lives

Team members from each division will email their Team Leader on the last day of each month. You have the opportunity to vote for one person per core value, but you must provide a specific example as to why you are voting for that person for that core value. You can vote for yourself. You do not have to nominate someone for each of the 4 core values.

The Team Leader will review all submissions and the person with the most nominations and best examples per team, will receive $228.00.

SABRE's Project 228 Award recognizing employees who exemplify core values.

To review in more detail, visit www.cultureczars.com

Mike Petsalis, CEO of Vircom, hands out statuettes of the *Star Trek* characters to everyone in the company who is "caught committing a core value" that month. These are vintage models found on Ebay. He has resisted handing out financial rewards, not because of budget, but because the statuettes are so highly valued by his team. One month, he didn't bother handing out the statuettes and the winners came to his office in protest. These seemingly simple things can take on great importance at little cost.

Vircom's statuettes, awarded by the CEO for employees who exemplify core values.

How will you create a means of recognition that ties your values to the company image? If you've given your CoreVals personas, you have all kinds of creative outlets. If not, delve deeper for ideas from the stories that generated your work, as well as those your work generated. Customer testimonials are gold mines of positive evidence. If you don't have those and your products or services are reviewed by the public—maybe on Amazon or such ratings websites as Yelp or TripAdvisor—you can read through the reviews for ideas. What do people like or think is unique about your organization? When you know what is already memorable, you can capitalize on that.

Now, let's take both the graphic display and engagement with your audience to its final rendition.

Showcase Your Core Values

How will you get eyes on your imagery? Again, you'll convene your core team to work out the final logistics. How many posters will you need? Where will you put them? Can you link them to other displays in your office space? At Lextech, our poster depicting *The Core* was prominently displayed around our offices and was adopted as the desktop wallpaper or home screen on many computers. We also dedicated one wall at the end of the hall to a mural of the personas.

Lextech's *The Core* poster displayed throughout its office spaces.

I loved that this was the first thing my prospective clients or employees saw in an online meeting or webinar. The fanciful expression of our CoreVals—with thoughtful, serious sentiments spelled out alongside the superheroes—told them exactly what it would be like to work with Lextech. How can your company make such a statement? Maybe you have a "wall of fame" with plaques for achievements the business has earned, or portraits of company leaders or employees of the month. Maybe your office has a dramatic architectural feature that draws the eye. Your CoreVals poster might make a nice centerpiece. Wherever you put it, find ways to draw attention to it and make it a focal point for office tours and group photos. If your team shares goodies on a regular basis, put the plate of jelly doughnuts on a table beneath the poster. When you take group photos, you know where to stage them. Keep the display prominent and attractive—don't let cobwebs, real or metaphorical, gather and dull the shine on your masterpiece.

Culture, Vision, Mission & Product Pride

The following values and behaviors define our culture. We believe that we are all accountable for our corporate values and for maintaining our culture and how we work together.

Proud & Passionate

We are proud of our mission to save and our global leading brands

We are passionate about our heroes, our team and our customers

Empowered

We evolve and solve

We are fired up

Prepared & Engaged

We plan for the best and prepare for the worst

We are condition yellow

Go the Extra Mile

We care and we do whatever it takes

We save lives

SABRE's core values displayed on cubicle cards.

There are many unconventional and creative ways to showcase your CoreVals. Recall the set of costumes my Lextech team gave me in honor of *The Core* characters. Besides my Captain Client getup, I had a Danny Deliver, UPS-like outfit, dressed up with a courier cape and a stuffed cheetah, indicating speed. Danny ostensibly carried our *Deliver Success* value to wherever it was needed most, in a hurry. I dressed up in ninja clothing to play teamwork alter-egos Tea

 To review in more detail, visit www.cultureczars.com

and Wok, and in Scottish garb to play Grow'n. Having no shame and an ample sense of humor, I happily donned a tight bustier when Passionista paid a visit to our Town Hall meeting. I begin each team meeting by telling a story about which employee was being honored with the CoreVal award that week. This was an effective way to make the core values thrive and encourage the behaviors that we wanted the team to emulate. These are examples of literally embodying core values in a visually memorable—albeit slightly nutty—way.

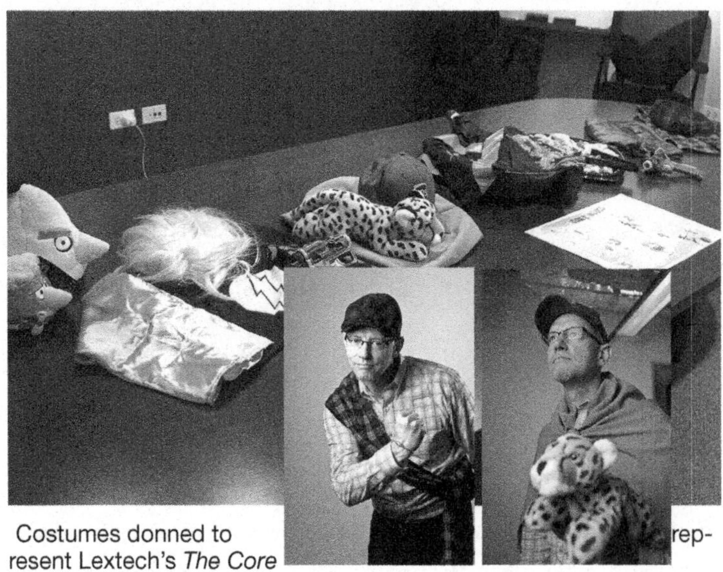

Costumes donned to represent Lextech's *The Core*

Finally, you'll want to dream up how to move your CoreVals and artwork in front of people outside the business. Your website home page or mobile app's welcome screen are easy, perpetual display sites. Promotional product companies can help you find giveaways—like pens, key fobs, or coffee mugs—on which to print some portion of your core values and graphic images.

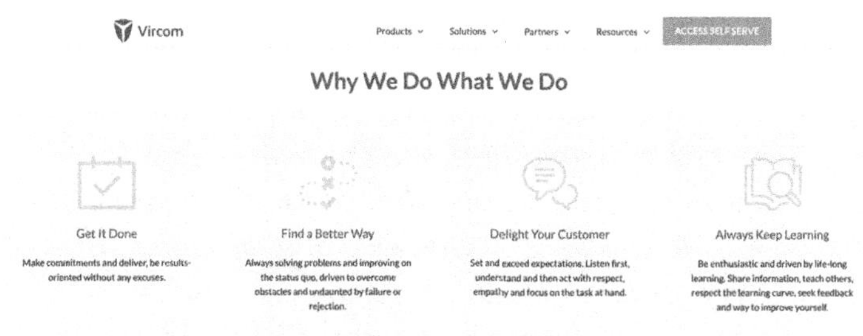

Vircom's CoreVals displayed on their website.

Lextech's CoreVals as seen on the company website.

Have fun with this part of the Culture Czars process. It may feel particularly satisfying because it uses both sides of your brain or because it connects the people inside your organization to the larger world. With your CoreVals created and displayed in the office, you are one step closer to the big day—your launch party.

Thoughts from a Culture Czar

"*Most of us frankly just pass [posters] by because we become numb to them. You must indeed figure out a way to live the values. That means that, for instance, in the awarding of rock stars every week, we asked every manager to submit a name.... That's one way we live it. The other way is to talk about it in team meetings.... Make sure you're having conversations about it, then ask the group to tell you examples of how we've been living our values.... You have to talk about [core values], and consistency is so critical in the success of any organization. Whether it's consistent in delivering our menu or producing a product. It's the same thing around core values. You have to be consistent in how you talk about them. You have to be good examples of them. Then, you have to continue to communicate them over and over and over again.... We may know what they are, but do we really practice them?*"

—DEE ROBINSON, FOUNDER AND CEO OF ROBINSON HILL

EXERCISE 4: DESIGN

We've walked through the steps that my company and consulting clients took to put their chosen CoreVals into words and pictures. Now, you try it. Complete the following tasks to use a theme, imagery, and company history to make your presentation memorable. Then decide how and where to present your company's core values to the world. Week 4 of your culture quest will be similar to Week 2—you can repeat it until you arrive at something that's just right. Consult the image below to see how we brought the Culture Czar's CoreVals alive.

CULTURE CZARS COREVALS

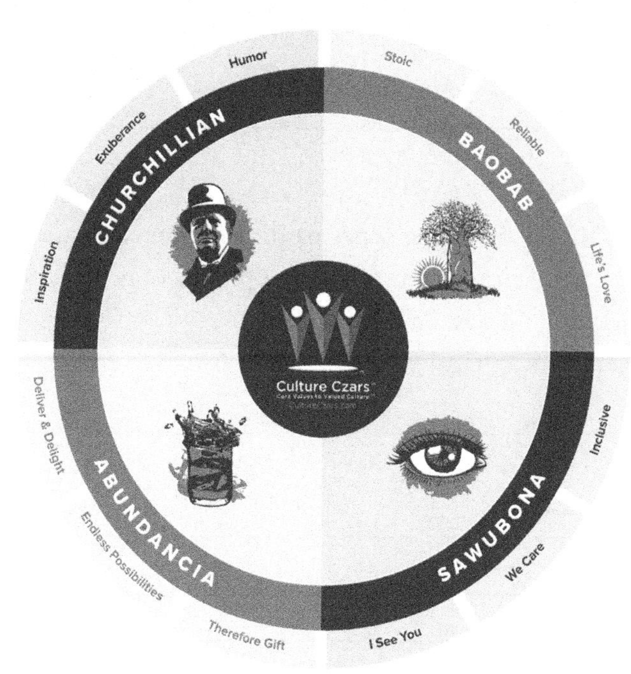

A. Use multimedia ideas to design a larger-than-life display for your CoreVals. Brainstorm with your team in the categories below.

PERSONAS/THEMES

Can you conceive a set of characters that embody your core values? Try using movie icons, personal heroes, or popular historical or fictional characters (such as Yoda, Mahatma Gandhi, Rosa Parks, or Sherlock Holmes). If personas don't work for you, try selecting a theme that evokes imagery (such as dawn, the ocean, or outer space).

____

____

____

IMAGES

What images fit the personas or themes you came up with? These can be custom illustrations or photos of people, places, historical buildings, or landmarks.

____

____

____

MUSIC

Now appeal to the sense of hearing by pairing your theme with a powerful song related to your core values. Popular music, classical pieces, anthems, or movie soundtracks can all stir emotions and have associations with your CoreVals. You can use this theme song at your launch party, meetings, and special events. This raises the fun quotient and makes people feel good! For example, SABRE began and ended their CoreVal launch event with "Start Me Up" by the Rolling Stones because the company's tagline incorporated one of the lines in the song, "Making grown men cry since 1975."

____

____

____

B. Revisit your company history to select stories that exemplify your core values. You can incorporate these into your launch party addresses, monthly awards, CoreVals poster, and other promotional opportunities.

COMPANY STORIES

____

____

____

MONTHLY AWARD

Award Name

____

____

Award Format (gift card, cash, etc.)

____

____

____

C. Bring the elements of your core values together through personas, images, stories, etc. Then list how you will display this poster or visual representation.

DISPLAY

Where will you put your main CoreVals posters? What collateral will you use to display CoreVals and imagery? (Such as your website, advertising, packaging, pocket cards, flyers, key fobs, costumes, etc.)

____

____

____

CHAPTER 5

Decree

'All hail! my own inspired Bard!
In me thy native Muse regard!
Nor longer mourn your fate is hard,
Thus poorly low!
I come to give you such reward,
As we bestow.

—ROBERT BURNS, THE VISION

THE MOMENT YOU ANNOUNCE your core values to your team, with all sincerity, is the point of no return—in a good way. It is the moment when you will accept the privilege and responsibility of being a Culture Czar. Like becoming a parent, leading a culture is a vocation that lasts for the lifetime of your organization, or at least for your tenure at its helm. If you have read this far, you are willing to take on that role and wear it like a superhero's cape. Do that and your culture will thrive.

Before that moment arrives, you will want some assurance that you will be heard and that your message will be well received. That type of respect and faith is rooted in trust. This is the bedrock that makes employees feel safe to work freely in a group. Does it exist in your organization? Some CEOs have trust issues that prevent them from relying on the very people who can best help them run the company. In some cases, simply clinging to old protocols can keep you from turning over tasks to people who can—and are quite willing to—do them well. Remember that your CoreVals will help you delegate, which will help you grow, because you can trust your reports to make decisions the same way you would.

Clinging to control is needlessly exhausting. According to Lumiere founder Kitsa Antonopoulos, it leaves you in the weeds, bogged down by details, and blocks progress. "I've seen a lot of companies not shift into growth because the decision maker is not able to trust the team and let others take care of things." She credits a regular meeting cycle for building and maintaining trust and holding people accountable to processes and schedules. Furthermore, these meetings offer continual opportunities to keep the company's core values in the forefront. It is likely that your CoreVals hinge on some of these elements. How could you claim to *Make it Work*, for example, if you are not accountable for your responsibilities? Suppose a clinical staff member is not completing the paperwork necessary for a client to receive treatment. That not only violates *Make it Work* and *You've Got This*, but it is not *Win-Win-Win* either. That's how easy it is to use CoreVals. Periodic meetings establish goals, deliverables, and deadlines. Should people fall short of those expectations, you can point to your core values to insist they elevate their standards.

Your CoreVals launch event will also be the initiator of a new meeting framework—one in which you will discuss and address issues *in light of the company's values and purpose.* This removes the type of personal overtones that lead to defensiveness and excuses. It's not, "Hey, Jeff. You failed our patients," but, "Please try harder to meet your objectives, Jeff, because we are all committed to Core Value Number X." This positive angle fits right in with the monthly award we talked about in Chapter 4. Instead of always pointing to those who fail to live up to company values, we can recognize people who consistently do, or who show instances of going above and beyond to do so. SABRE CEO, David Nance, points out, "It's easier to be critical of someone than to commend them for a great job. That's just human nature. It goes a long way when you acknowledge people for doing good things. It makes them want to repeat them and they feel integral to the team—more invested." This level of engagement reached by regular acknowledgement builds the trust you need to delegate your responsibilities and the trust your team needs to work together. Periodic meetings provide a chance to publicly acknowledge work that is congruent with company values and interests.

When I first walked into one small company, its twenty-five employees had just made it through the winter by working sixty hours per week. It was the only way the company kept afloat; twenty-five multiplied by sixty, multiplied by their hourly pay rate, was what the company needed to break even. When all you do is keep breathing, it sucks the enjoyment out of every day. At that business, no one liked the work they were doing, they didn't like their customers, and they barely tolerated each other.

Situations like this—in which there is no sense of teamwork or community, and in which work is focused on day-to-day survival rather than future goals—leave no room for a healthy culture. Because a healthy culture doesn't exist, neither is there a purpose for showing up, other than getting a paycheck. Even then, poor productivity and shaky financial standing may mean payrolls are missed and the one remaining promise to employees is broken.

When workers are disenfranchised in this way, the only fix is to create a defined culture they can relate to, and a purpose to their work that makes them feel valued for making meaningful contributions. These measures also tell employees how they fit into the larger scheme of business and how they can do their jobs well. Otherwise, they may live in fear of getting fired. As most business leaders know, people in that state will work just hard enough to stave off a pink slip. That's no way for a company, a culture, or an individual to thrive.

When workers are disenfranchised in this way, the only fix is to create a defined culture they can relate to, and a purpose to their work that makes them feel valued for making meaningful contributions.

When employees are included in weekly or monthly meetings in which expectations are laid out and committed to, they know what it takes to succeed in their jobs. Only then can they excel. This is why we include core value talks in every meeting, and why the Culture Czars system emphasizes a consistent meeting cycle. It makes the CoreVals integration automatic.

Use Core Values to Inspire Faith and Trust

This doesn't mean you can only establish teamwork and community when your business first opens its doors. Far from it. In fact, "broken" cultures have the most to gain from a formal CoreVals launch and integration with planning sessions and meetings. For instance, what happens when overwork displaces teamwork? How about a culture in which the employees' welfare is way down the list or when sexual harassment or some other social problem taints internal relations? Let's consider how core values can resurrect such faltering cultures.

We hear in the news about big organizations that are rocked with revelations of sexual harassment that threaten their viability. Oftentimes the behaviors have persisted for long periods of time and suddenly come to light. This happens because communication channels are segmented, and when people speak, they are not heard. Take Uber, the ride-hailing service corporation. In 2017, a female engineer reported being sexually harassed by a manager and being threatened with termination if she pursued reparations. Investigation revealed that management knew of this predicament and did nothing. A pattern of such behavior was discovered, and eventually, more than twenty Uber employees were dismissed in connection with the issue.

These cover-ups can happen because a culture of enabling and complicity exists at the top tiers of an organization. To Uber's credit, in addition to adopting specific ways of preventing and reporting sexual harassment, management revisited and revised the core values that contributed to the faulty culture. In my opinion, the previous values had been left open to misinterpretation. Indeed, Uber's current CEO, Dara Khosrowshahi, admits that some values, like *Toe-stepping* and *Principled confrontation*, while meant to allow any employee to speak truth to power, was considered by some as license to walk all over people without consequences. The investigator brought in to root out corruption in the company called on

Uber to axe *Toe-stepping* and other questionable values that might justify bad behavior. Suppose you worked for Uber and were left to interpret what *Always be hustlin'* alluded to. See what I mean?

This is why the Culture Czars process includes the Describe phase, which we covered in Chapter 3. When you clarify what your necessarily shortened core values really mean, you fill some of the cracks that less-ethical people would slip through. While Uber's new list of core values doesn't outright state, *Don't sexually harass people or threaten to fire the ones who report it*, they do include, *We do the right thing* and *We celebrate differences*. I guess that includes respecting individuals' physical sovereignty.

Is there still too much wiggle room? For one thing, the company is calling their list *norms* not *values,* the rationale being that they are subject to change. More telling is how these priorities are handled by the company leaders. According to a James Kerr article for *Inc.* magazine, CEO Khosrowshahi withheld news of a 2017 data breach that put more than fifty million Uber customers at risk for months before notifying them.[14] How does that square with doing the right thing?

It remains to be seen whether Uber's new normal will repair the torn fabric of its culture. As you can see, just having core values posted on a wall won't cut it. Expecting employees to interpret them correctly can cause terrible problems. Issuing value statements that executives do not heed is no way to convince the rest of the company to adhere to them. This is why *you* must be the one to announce your CoreVals, model them, and refer to them over and over again, in daily

---

14 James Kerr, "Uber: What Happened to Your Core Values," *Inc. Magazine,* December 4, 2017, https://www.inc.com/james-kerr/uber-what-happened-to-your-core-values.html.

huddles, weekly conferences, and monthly meetings—and any other chance you get.

Plan Your Launch Party

That brings us to the incredible promise inherent in the launch of your new culture. If business or office dynamics are not healthy, this can be a game changer. If things are going well, it will only get better from here. You're almost ready to write the agenda for the big day. In the last workbook exercise, you established some of the window dressing you will use—artwork, personas, theme songs. You also created a form of monthly recognition to link to your CoreVals and decided on memorabilia, such as key chains, cards, and coffee mugs, that will keep your well-chosen words in people's minds. It's time to finalize the details involved in your core values initiation to ensure you're ready to count down and blast off at your launch party.

You should have two different groups who will help you lock in these details. First, get your leadership team to iron out the meeting frequencies and ways to tie core values with the issues of the day. Second, round up your Cultural Czars—they will play a key role in ensuring your core value message is well received.

Yes, I continue to stress how crucial it is for staff to hear the CoreVal decree from their leader. We must also form a bridge from senior management to employees at all other levels. Top-down modeling—walking the walk—is easy to accept. Telling people how values inform their labor, not so much. Your people won't have to take it on faith if they also hear the same thing from their peers. You will want to identify czars throughout your organization who get it and are eager to spread the word.

Sit down with a group of them beforehand and get their input on how the new values relate to their time with the company. This is meant to demonstrate some continuity amid the changes to come. Ask them to relate anecdotes, either of past failures that could have been avoided with the support of core values, or of future hopes that can be improved with CoreVals.

Then move on to the fun aspect of the big day. Plan the music, food, decorations, and any unique ideas for making your CoreVals rollout memorable. Decide how big a group you can accommodate and whether any guest speakers will add weight to the presentation. Take names of volunteers to speak at the event. We'll focus on your keynote address in Chapter 6. Use the workbook pages that follow to decide the who, what, when, where, and why of the event. Then, start the countdown.

Thoughts from a Culture Czar

"*One of the joys I have of being…a business owner and a CEO is I get to pick the people I want to work with. I want to work with awesome, great people who share the same values and share the same type of fun working experience that I want.…Nowadays we spend so much of our time working, so why not make it fun? I think when people have a place they want to come into,…where they enjoy their coworker's company,…then it doesn't make work, work. It makes it fun and a pleasurable activity. At the end of the day, when you're engaged and you're having fun, that will have an impact on profitability.*"

–SONNY BALANI,
CEO OF BALINI CUSTOM CLOTHIERS

EXERCISE 5: DECREE

You will repeat the message you deliver at your CoreVals launch again and again. Finalize a meeting cycle that will become an auto-pilot platform for keeping your company's core values at the top of everyone's mind.

A. Plan your ongoing meeting rhythm. How will you incorporate core values into each of your meetings?

Daily Huddles

____

____

Weekly Team Meetings

____

____

Weekly Management Meetings

____

____

Townhall/All-hands Monthly Meetings (in which awards are distributed)

____

____

B. Plan your launch event. Identify the details and your Culture Czars who will serve as peer liaisons.

When

____

____

Where

____

____

Why (your personal motivation for addressing culture)

____

____

What (visuals and handouts)

____

____

Who (czars and other guest speakers)

____

____

How (any other details)

____

____

CHAPTER 6

Dictate

And when the bard, or hoary sage,
Charm or instruct the future age,
They bind the wild poetic rage
In energy;
Or point the inconclusive page
Full on the eye.

—ROBERT BURNS, THE VISION

CREATING YOUR CORE VALUES is best done cooperatively as a team. However, the speech that will dictate what defines your company is best led by the leader. If not, your employees will wonder, *if you can't say it, how can you do it?* You can certainly involve your senior leadership team, Culture Czars, and other associates who contributed to the effort. You'll all be involved in this phase, but the founder, owner, or CEO should lead the address.

Picture the scene, you've called the whole company together for an announcement. You have unfurled a banner with your core values emblazoned across it, proclaiming your collective beliefs in word and deed. You have invited staff members and dignitaries to the microphone to share their stories of the organization's most memorable and positive impacts. Then it's your turn. Here's some suggestions on how to best create a CoreVals address.

Your CoreVals address should be:

- Inclusive
- Inspiring
- Evergreen

You will have many occasions to repeat your address, but only one chance to make a memorable first impression on your most important audience.

Keep It Real

For a leader desiring to make an emotional connection, a great way to build the trust, affinity, and buy-in you are looking for is to be vulnerable and transparent. In an interview for the Culture Czar podcast series, Todd Smart from Chicago Traction Center says, "People trust others who are willing to be vulnerable, so if you're prancing around in your office with your ego and your self-importance and your bulletproof-ness and never show the soft underbelly, it's really difficult for others to trust [you]."

In *The Culture Code,* Daniel Coyle writes, "Vulnerability doesn't come after trust—it precedes it. Leaping into the unknown, when done alongside others, causes the solid ground of trust to materialize beneath our feet."[15] If you haven't been a vulnerable leader up until this point, it's okay. As Coyle points out, once you start being vulnerable, be assured that you are building trust with your team. One effective way to show vul-

15 Daniel Coyle, *The Culture Code: The Secrets of Highly Successful Groups* (New York: Random House, 2018), 107.

nerability at this moment would be to tell a story about a time when you worked for an employer whose culture was weak or nonexistent, and how that made you feel. Or you could relate a story behind one or two of the core values you are about to present. Make it personal and don't be afraid to get emotional. Appeal to your people as individuals and as a group. Strike a tone that is both high-minded and down-to-earth.

Sound impossible? Try reading this aloud:

> We the people, in order to form a more perfect union, establish justice, ensure domestic tranquility, provide for the common defense, promote the general welfare, and secure the blessings of liberty to ourselves and our posterity, do ordain and establish this Constitution for the United States of America.

That is, of course, the preamble to the U.S. Constitution, the greatest expression of core values in our country's history. If that document were a verbal speech, it would hit all the right notes. We're all in this together. These are things we can all endorse and conditions that should infinitely persevere for the benefit of future generations.

After I became an American citizen and adopted the U.S. Constitution as part of my personal credo, it occurred to me that this document serves the same purpose as my old clubhouse rules. How would three hundred million Americans—or people in any country—coexist without a shared constitution? These laws are nothing more than rules based on a set of values. We all know what they mean and what they stand for. And just as we couldn't harmoniously coexist without them, I don't know how any company operates without values. They are like a compass, a true north, that provide a mantra for how to live and work together. What you will say matters deeply, almost as much as what you will do afterward, because words are just words if not supported by the right actions.

What you will say matters deeply, almost as much as what you will do afterward, because words are just words if not supported by the right actions.

A Most Important Speech

You are ready to dictate your CoreVals address—to yourself, and to your people. This is not a one-off deal. It's a speech you will give as often as appropriate to build connection and trust with your team. Onboarding new hires? Check. Project debriefing? Check. Working with a new stakeholder, whether a customer, partner, supplier, or shareholder? You bet. You may want to pen an in-depth version plus a couple of abbreviated editions. In the door-knocking, canvassing world, these spiels are called your "rap"—the facts and rationales you present to bring people on board as you ask for signatures, donations, or support. That's basically what you'll be doing with your core values pep talks.

Among the elements you'll want to include in your CoreVals address are:

- Each value, along with its descriptive behaviors
- Company stories that relate to each value
- How building culture fits in with the arc of your company's history
- Anecdotes about how you got interested in culture
- Who helped you in your current effort
- Cautionary tales about what happens when companies lose sight of their purpose (See our blog at www.cultureczars.com for examples).
- Company goals that will benefit from basing decisions on CoreVals
- How values will help employees enjoy autonomy, mastery, and purpose
- How values will increase the company's market standing and stability
- How you, personally, will benefit from the effort
- Your pledge to leading a culture that is consistent with the CoreVals
- How this small investment will yield high returns

Although your audience might seem to be captive and easily influenced, remember that you will give this address in other venues to other stakeholders. It should be just as relevant to anyone as it will be to your staff. Keep the content universal and authentically delivered. Again, core values cannot rest on wishful thinking. They must be attainable and supportable, as continually and consistently as possible, by the organization's leaders, in order to motivate others to succeed in those behaviors. This is where you come in. Your speech is not just a speech. It's a challenge to yourself as well as to others.

Thoughts from a Culture Czar

"*For some reason in business, we're told not to talk about our feelings. Like they're separate, put [them] in a box and you can never take them out. But what I learned…[was] the more you are in tune with your emotions, the more emotionally intelligent you are, [and] the greater results you'll get as a leader or as a CEO."*"

–DAN HEUERTZ,
CEO OF THE PREFERRED GROUP

EXERCISE 6: DICTATE

Keep your wider audience in mind when composing your CoreVals address. It should appeal to current staff, new employees, vendors, customers, investors, shareholders, and other stakeholders. Work below on some rough ideas for your speech. Ensure your words become deeds. Create a mechanism to hold yourself accountable for putting culture first, even as it projects into the future.

If you get stuck, need examples, or want more resources to help draft your address, visit www.cultureczars.com/the-culture-fix-book.

A. Write down ideas, themes, elements, and anecdotes to include in your speech. Take this rough sketch to your voice recorder, computer, or pen and paper to expand it into a compelling core values address. Then edit it down to its essence, revising language for its greatest impact.

____

____

____

B. Schedule a regular time and place to evaluate your personal commitment to core values and promoting culture. How can you make periodic check-ins satisfying and meaningful to yourself?

PART THREE

DRIVE

Execute in Line with Core Values

- ✓ Devise
- ✓ Deliver
- ✓ Determine

CHAPTER 7

Devise

To lower orders are assign'd
The humbler ranks of human-kind,
The rustic bard, the laboring farm servant,
The artisan;
All choose, as various they are inclined,
The various man.

—ROBERT BURNS, THE VISION

HOW WILL YOU HIRE, unhire, and evaluate to preserve your core values? How will you design and document the fundamental work your company does in line with these ideals? How will you bring both together and set people up to succeed within your operational framework? You'll do it by putting in place Core People Processes—the hiring, unhiring, and evaluating protocols based on CoreVals. You will also rely on CoreWorkflows—the overarching company workflow or master process. These two major business procedures can make or break a culture.

These practices impact the team and are especially effective as you grow and add people to your roster. It's important to have a process to remove, or unhire, people when they don't fit the task or the team to preserve the harmony and greater good of the group. They will also help you acknowledge superior work without bias. Seize these golden opportunities to relieve yourself from having to make judgment calls on a case-by-case basis. As seasoned entrepreneur, CEO, and founder of Chicago Traction Center, Todd Smart, shared with me in a podcast interview, core values not only help with the selection of candidates, but they also strengthen the dynamic between employee and employer, and provide important opportunities to fortify the existing culture:

> A quarterly conversation is a one-on-one between all bosses and employees, where culture is a primary piece of the conversation. I look at our core values when I'm sitting…with one of my direct reports and I ask…"In which one of our core values do you have the most room for improvement?" I also pick the core value in which I have the most room for improvement, and then we share our answers. This is a boss-to-employee relationship filled with love, trust, and respect. Then we get to have a quality conversation about what they could do better…and what I could do as their boss to help or support them in rising up around that core value. Most organizations don't have a loving, direct [approach toward] this. However, if you're about to fire somebody because they don't fit your culture—yet you've never offered them open-communication coaching about how to get there—shame on you.

When we apply protocols evenly, we increase our integrity and invite trust. Our job becomes easier because people place confidence in us and accept our authority. As Simon Sinek puts it in *Start With Why*, "Those who lead are able to do so because those who follow trust that the decisions made at the top have the best interest of the group at heart. In turn, those who trust work hard because they feel like they are working for something bigger than themselves."[16] By hiring, unhiring, and evaluating in accord with CoreVals, we establish and further the company's—and our employees'—purpose, as well as preserve and enhance our culture.

The case-by-case method, on the other hand, drains your resolve. Not wanting to "waste" interview time, you might be tempted to hire an imperfect fit. Not wanting to enter yet another difficult conversation, you might avoid or delay unhiring an unsatisfactory employee. Letting the wrong person stay only helps that one person—and you may not even be doing them a service. Meanwhile, you harm many people, as well as your business image and prospects. The truth is, you are only as good as your worst employee.

The truth is, you are only as good as your worst employee.

What if the company has an endemic cultural problem? How do you change the culture if the environment is toxic, especially if you need to fix it quickly? The answer is to change the people. Maybe some of the people, or maybe a lot of the people. Maybe the changes are at the leadership level or maybe they are in the lower ranks—or both. That may be the only way to truly achieve change, especially if it needs to be done quickly. That's why large organizations are so hard to change: there may be too many people involved.

Meaghan Mullgardt, SABRE's CEO, mentioned in an interview for this book that staff also benefit from that consistency.

---

16 Simon Sinek, *Start With Why: How Great Leaders Inspire Everyone to Take Action* (New York: Penguin Press, 2009), 85.

"Having the values as a guide to hire and unhire helps people who are struggling to realize their mistakes and how they need to change if they want to remain in their jobs." Knowing what defines success in a job description is essential to hitting goals and moving toward bonuses or promotions. Meaghan also notes the psychological outcomes that clear standards have on staff members who reach difficult crossroads: "It makes everything more sensitive because people know what is expected of them." This shows respect. She further points out that CoreVal standards bring clarity to assessing good employee fits. They make it easier to determine who does not want to be part of the defined culture. Then the only questions are, *Should we bring or keep them on board? Or have we completely exhausted all of those avenues and we have to let them go?*

Kitsa Antonopoulos of Lumiere also appreciates the more specific direction that values-based hiring allows. After narrowing the field, she reaches out to candidates through a video call to get an initial feeling about fit. In addition to paying attention to her first impression and gut feeling, Kitsa is applying an element of the CoreScore—a numeric measurement that indicates the degree to which employees and teams work in concert with CoreVals—according to the following scale:

CoreScore Scale for Fit:

- Do they/would they fit all of the time? = 3
- Do they/would they fit most of the time? = 2
- Do they/would they fit some of the time? = 1
- Do they/would they fit none of the time? = 0

The CoreScore is easily applied to both current employees and new candidates applying to join the team. A low score obviously means the candidate in question is not right for the role. Kitsa credits this litmus test for creating trust and building a culture of accountability. It also eliminates the guesswork from interviewing prospects and evaluating staff performance, while providing a scale that removes some subjectivity, shows trends, and gets more accurate over time. "Now I automatically do it," she says. "I hire people and ask, *do they fit?*" In her therapy practice, hiring for cultural integration is the priority. "Lots of people are trained as good therapists—they're highly educated and good at what they do—but the character they bring to their work is the biggest deal for us."

We recommend regularly measuring your current employees on the same simple scale as the one below. Your Culture Czars will, of course, earn a perfect score! Here is another example of an effective CoreScore measure:

	CoreVal				**Total**	
Values	**1**	**2**	**3**	**4**	**(12)**	**Action**
Sam	3	2	3	4	**12**	Share with Sam
Marty	2	2	2	3	**9**	Provide feedback/ coach
Lauren	2	1	1	2	**6**	Provide feedback/ coach

The employee represents this core value:

0 = None of the time　　2 = Most of the time
1 = Some of the time　　3 = All of the time

Color coding affords instant recognition. Assign a red, yellow, green status to the CoreScore, and it quickly becomes evident who your rock stars are (green), who you could consider hiring, and who needs to be unhired (red) or not considered for employment. In the example above, Sam is a rock star and probable Culture Czar. Marty is solid enough, but Lauren needs to be on a watch list and also provided with feedback and training. You hope the CEO and leaders are all going to score perfectly, but this is not always the case. Scores that are less than ideal do, however, provide the opportunity for introspection and culture-powered conversation.

Whenever I score a large group of associates, there are usually at least one or two "reds" at the bottom of the chart. The CoreScore makes it really clear and validates whatever feeling you had in your gut about an individual, especially when benchmarked against a group of their peers. It's only fair to give these individuals immediate feedback in a personal conversation, referencing the CoreVals. They are probably not feeling comfortable in the culture anyway. Why? Because they don't fit and won't feel like a valued member of the group who is making a meaningful contribution. After giving the feedback, quickly decide if they are capable and willing to turn it around or if you need to make the decision for them. In some cases, those who are poor fits self-select and exit on their own.

At Lextech, we scored candidates on values, and found we had more hits than misses in our hiring. I remember considering one prospect in light of our value *Passion & Energy*. During the video interview, I thought this energetic individual was going to jump out of the screen onto my desk. Years later, after hiring him, he is still a tour de force at the company.

On the other hand, I had one client who just couldn't bring himself to unhire an employee who was consistently scoring in the red. She had been loyal through difficult times, and he didn't want to lose her expertise. Yet, she was a huge drain on energy and time for this small team. This individual's negative attitude colored everything she did and seeped into other people's consciousness. The irony was that the company's first CoreVal was *Positive attitude.* Still, inordinate amounts of time were spent discussing this one employee, instead of focusing on the high performers who did fit the culture. What effect do you think the lack of action had on the credibility of the CEO in the eyes of the rest of the team?

Furthermore, in the early years at Waer Systems, we had a cultural misfit who was starting to drag the team down. This was another negative person who wasn't a bad performer, just a cultural antagonist. The friction he caused did an amazing amount of damage to morale and productivity. I wasn't sure how to go about the unhiring process, so I decided to start by discussing our CoreVals in a closed-door meeting. I went through them, one by one, reiterating that the people who thrived at Waer Systems were individuals who felt like they were a fit with our stated values. Every now and then, I would pause to let one sink in, or simply ask, "Do you feel like these values resonate with you?" Finally, to my surprise, he volunteered, "Maybe I should be looking to work elsewhere." With relief, I quickly confirmed this sentiment, and we were able to amicably discuss his transition.

Your CoreVals will help you make the tough calls, and using the CoreScore will ensure that you do so without rancor or personal bias. Once the "red" CoreScores are no longer on the team, you will notice a palpable turnaround in the group dynamic and wish you had done it sooner. Depending on the size of the team, it is possible for a company to get to a place where the team has no "reds." Companies achieve this all the time. When they do, it feels amazing, teamwork is effortless, and the company is cranking on all cylinders.

This is your goal. Wherever you look across the company, things will be going well, and people will be enjoying their work. You'll be free to concentrate *on* your business, not *in* your business, and you'll have time to do the things you're good at that fortify—rather than drain—your energy.

Core People Processes: Consistent Hiring, Unhiring, and Evaluating

It takes a lifetime to learn what makes people tick. Being able to weed out certain traits or proclivities is a great time and worry saver in the hiring process. The same goes for unhiring. In addition, there are other intricacies of the hiring process to consider apart from the cultural aspects, such as HR requirements, technical abilities, and work experience. This section does not make any attempt to address all the aspects of a hiring process, just the ones that pertain to cultural fit. Try using the basic framework of the Culture Czar steps below as part of your Core People Process.

1. Narrow the pool of candidates before you begin selection by using an applied analytics traits assessment such as Culture Index, which will provide a match between your ideal candidate and the hard-wired traits of all the applicants. I strongly recommend this tool, not only for recruiting, but also for managing existing team members. You only need to interview

those that are a close fits, thus eliminating a lot of unnecessary work reviewing poor-fit resumes.

Check my website at www.cultureczars.com/the-culture-fix-book for an introduction to the Culture Index tool.

2. Hold quick online interviews using a tool like Zoom or Skype. Face-to-face video conferencing provides a better opportunity to help you judge character and value fit. This will qualify or disqualify candidates before the next round: in-person interviews.
3. Hold on-site interviews with the hiring manager, a representative from leadership, and a panel of at least two experienced Culture Czars. You should be able to trust them to interview on the company's behalf, in line with core values, using behavioral and scenario-based questions.
4. Finally, before a formal offer is extended, have some of the candidates' would-be peers take them to dinner, where they can interact outside the office and in a more informal setting. At this stage, they may feel that they've got the job and relax. What do the candidates reveal about their true nature in these circumstances?

Let's go through these steps in more detail. After the initial evaluation and a narrowing of the candidate list, some folks make it to the next round, and we take a deeper dive into their cultural fit. This should be done by different team members from round one and be supported by an unbiased application of the CoreScore. Similar to a behavioral interview, ask a set of prescribed interview questions that you use for every candidate. This session should be led by at least two members of your existing team, so that when one is asking the questions, the other is observing and taking notes. They should score separately and compare their findings afterward. I am not saying this is easy to do, and it is certainly not foolproof. With practice, however, you will hone the questions and the listening skills and get better at selecting candidates who are more likely to fit the job and needs of the group.

Set the tone by connecting in person with your top candidates, whom you interviewed by phone or video, and who achieved a pass level on the CoreScore. Let them know they did well and that you're excited to get to know them better. To put them at ease, show them around the office, grab a coffee, and joke with them a bit. Meanwhile, be alert for expressions of *their* values and subtle, nonverbal cues about their character. Make sure your printed CoreVals are not in sight—you'll reveal them later, in a subsequent set of questions, where the candidate can actually read them. Begin by asking open-ended questions that get the candidate talking. Many entrepreneurs, including myself, have effectively deployed the strategies that Geoff Smart and Randy Street describe in their book, *Who: The A Method for Hiring*. These include: Build a scorecard; Source candidates; Conduct up to five types of interviews; Make a decision; and Sell.[17] These work well, but more can be done to determine whether a candidate really is a culture fit or not. I favor working through these questions and then diving deeper. Entrepreneurs will often say they hire for cultural fit, but when I ask "How?" I get blank stares and a vague reference to gut-feel.

17 Geoff Smart and Randy Street, *Who* (New York: Random House, 2008).

Having gathered some information, transition to the cultural interview: "What values are most important to you?" Spend some time and really get them talking and opening up. Follow up with more questions that dig deeper, based on what you are hearing. Pick up on the nuances and challenge them. You are listening for a match between what they volunteer and the qualities that you are looking for. My friend, Tim Heitmann, CEO of Double Good, documents the process. He and his team keep a copy of their CoreVals in front of them and make check marks by the pertinent value each time they hear a match. They add these up later.

Next, move on to scenario-based questions that begin with, "Let's say you find yourself in this situation...." Choose real-life examples that actually happened at your company. The stories we collected earlier in the Discover process make great fodder for this. You already know one correct answer from what actually happened. How do your candidates' responses align with your outcome and your values? Compile two or three of these scenario questions for each of your CoreVals. Build a spreadsheet and put the questions in the first column, the *ideal* answers in the next column, and spaces to capture their answers next to that. Over time, you will build up data that helps you hone the skill of interviewing for culture fit.

Consider an example specific to Lumiere Children's Therapy: in the panel interview, we put the candidate in a hypothetical conversation with a parent who is expressing specific desires about what they want their child to obtain from treatment—outcomes that Lumiere refers to as "magic moments." We want the candidate to show how they might fulfill the parent's wishes, demonstrating their understanding of Lumiere's value that states, *Family goals are our goals.* The ideal answer earns a CoreScore value of three or four. If, instead, they try to muscle the parent to a different point of view, citing their training and experience to insist that they know what is best for the child, they will fall short. This gets a CoreScore value of one or zero. When you later reveal the CoreVals, go back to the question and give the prospect a chance to comment on their answer again. Do they get it now? Or are they defensive? Apply these steps to all of your values, and see what the final CoreScore is. Unfortunately it is hard to share actual scenario-based questions from clients because they consider them to be strategically important, but you will find some examples on our website.

Those who score well will have met you, the Human Resources manager, the hiring manager, the Culture Czars, and some functional experts. Next comes the final interview and then, dinner with potential coworkers. These are the people who would be working closely with the candidate and who have the most to gain or lose. They can provide the ultimate assessment of whether your prospect will likely fit and enhance the team, or at least not detract from the dynamic that is working so well.

All of the interviewers should assemble to review the consolidated CoreScores and meet-and-greet results the next day. Make the decision, extend the offer, and make that new hire's first day memorable. Do what it takes to help them feel included and safe in the group. After all, they are the latest recruit into a special clubhouse.

CoreWorkflows: Setting Your Team Up for Success

Your company has probably established procedures to lend consistency to the way work flows through the business, so that you follow protocols and your success repeats. You probably need several of these for the different streams of activities within your enterprise, but for the purpose of supporting culture, we are most interested in an overarching umbrella process that headlines all others. It is particularly important in a business-to-business (B2B) environment. There is no point in building a high-performing team and then sabotaging them with crazy business goals, nonsensical procedures, or clumsy, undocumented workflows. Great people on a great team, working within an efficient, documented, and well-planned business process, are the keys to productivity. I call this your CoreWorkflow—the overarching company workflow or master process.

Your CoreWorkflow Should:

- Outline the major steps the company or organization takes in the process of delivering its work.
- Help every employee know where they fit in the big picture, how their work connects to everyone else, and what contribution they make to the whole.
- Provide an overview to customers and clients that tells them what to expect when they work with you.
- Contain none of the company's competitive secrets. It can, therefore, be displayed publicly.
- Tie into the CoreVals.

Below is an example of a CoreWorkflow from Matrix4, a plastics design and manufacturing house focused on the consumer market that I consulted with. CEO Patricia Miller had to reinvent everything about Matrix4 after taking over the company, including the processes she used to run the business. Note the way Patricia combined her CoreVals and CoreWorkflow and then went further by depicting them graphically.

Steps 1 to 3; **BRAND;** MATRIX4, Reputation, Community (People First)

Steps 4 to 6; **RELATIONSHIP;** Leads, Referrals, RFQs (People First)

Steps 7 to 9; **SOLUTION;** Expertise, Proposal, Timing (Make Meaningfully)

Steps 10 to 12; **ONBOARD**; Kickoff, Details, Project Management (Make Meaningfully)

Steps 13 to 15; **EXECUTE**; Buy, Train, Make (Communicate Purposefully)

Steps 16 to 18; **DELIVER**; Pack, Ship, On Time On Quality Every Time, (OTOQET) (Communicate Purposefully)

M4 CoreWorkflow

PEOPLE FIRST

BRAND
- MATRIX 4
- Reputation
- Community

RELATIONSHIP
- Leads
- Referrals
- RFQs

MAKE MEANINGFULLY

SOLUTION
- Expertise
- Proposal
- Timing

ONBOARD
- Kick off
- Details
- Project Mgt

COMMUNICATE PURPOSEFULLY

EXECUTE
- Buy
- Train
- Make

DELIVER
- Pack
- Ship
- OTOQET

DELIVER A POSITIVE CUSTOMER EXPERIENCE AT EVERY TOUCHPOINT

Matrix4's CoreWorkflow

It can be quick and easy for you and your team to devise your CoreWorkflow and merge it with your CoreVals. If you already have documented processes for each of the work streams in the business, this will knit them all together at a high level. Once you have written out the key steps using carefully chosen, all-encompassing words, group and organize them in a logical sequence—always bearing in mind your core values. Your goal is to integrate your core values and CoreWorkflow into a statement that is uniquely yours, as seen in Lextech's CoreWorkflow below.

Lextech's CoreWorkflow

To review in more detail, visit www.cultureczars.com

The Master LexGuide—as we called our CoreWorkflow—was the overarching workflow document, the umbrella to each of the individual workflows. Note that each workflow title had a value statement or intention, which provided a useful summary of the purpose of each workflow. Each workflow also had both a detailed process description (not shown), and a poster that was displayed in the relevant team room. For an example, see the Design LexGuide below that focused on the values exemplified by Captain Client and Danny Deliver. Each workflow had its own value emphasis pertinent to each team.

Lextech's Design LexGuide

Now, a few words about the Client LexGuide shown below. This was a great moment for my partner and me because this initiative was led by our team. We had not even conceived of a Client LexGuide. Our team wanted a guide that would call out the values of our relationship with clients. As these values were important to all of us, we were delighted to immortalize them into their own workflow.

In this moment, my partner and I knew our Core Values had taken on a new momentum because this was an entirely team-led initiative.

Lextech's Client LexGuide

Every business succeeds through disciplined action. Winging it cannot be sustained. Following standard procedures that tie into core values is an easy way to instill discipline and accountability in your staff. Once you have devised the protocols, you'll want to assess if they are working as planned. Google takes pride in saying, *We measure everything.* How else will you know for sure? Creating protocols and a numeric rating system will allow you to hire and unhire, monitor work flows, and evaluate employees consistently and objectively.

Thoughts from a Culture Czar

“*Culture eats strategy. You can have the best strategy in the world. You can have all these KPIs and... metrics that you want to meet, but if your employees are not in alignment with your vision, they will create their own culture. They'll invent their own way of doing things.... You have to really figure out who those people are, your engaged employees....Being that it's a candidate driven market...they can pick up and go very quickly, and you're going to lose a leader within your organization. It's difficult to replace those people....If fifty to seventy percent of your employees are disengaged, then you, as a company, are losing a lot of money. Calls aren't being made, things are being dropped. There's no follow up...Doors are spinning at 5 o'clock. That's a terrible person to have as an employee.*”

– BEJAN DOURAGHY,
FOUNDER AND CEO OF ARTISAN TALENT

EXERCISE 7: DEVISE

A. Devise Core People Processes—Discerning what people's values are and whether they are in sync with your company's CoreVals are crucial to effective hiring and unhiring. Complete the following sections to establish some guidelines.

HIRING FOR FIT

Compose questions that you and your team will use for all prospects during the interview process. Draw on company lore and the stories you documented earlier to come up with scenario-based questions and answers. Draft general and role-specific questions that probe for personal values.

Question 1

____

____

Question 2

____

____

Question 3

____

____

HOW AND WHEN TO UNHIRE

Get one of your czars to help you role-play an exit conversation with a poorly performing employee. Use your company's CoreVals to evaluate the employee's behavior. Run through the scenario a couple times, improving any trouble spots and solidifying your technique.

B. Use the CoreScore—Determine a schedule for evaluating your employees via their CoreScores. Also decide when you will rate your cultural health. Both of these rating efforts should result in concrete actions.

Use the tables below to rate your team and your company's overall culture by department.

EMPLOYEE CORESCORE

Name	CoreVal 1	CoreVal 2	CoreVal 3	CoreVal 4	Total (12)	Action

CoreScore scale:

- Do they/would they fit this core value all of the time? = 3
- Do they/would they fit this core value most of the time? = 2
- Do they/would they fit this core value some of the time? = 1
- Do they/would they fit this core value none of the time? = 0

TEAM CORESCORE

Rating teams against the CoreVals can also be revealing and drive decision making. Try rating a team that is not performing as well as you would like and see what you learn.

Date: Last Qtr.	CoreVal				Total	
TEAM	**1**	**2**	**3**	**4**	**(20)**	**Action**
Marketing	5	3	3	1	**12**	Discuss/share this evaluation with the marketing team.

C. Devise your CoreWorkflow—Work with your team to outline the ten to twenty steps that make up the end-to-end process of how work flows through the company. Summarize each step with just a word or two. Gather your detailed workflows, and make sure there is consistency between these and the CoreWorkflow that you just devised.

Assemble the steps into three to five logical groupings, using graphics to depict momentum. Is the workflow linear or circular, does it flow left to right or from the top, down? Or does some other representation work for your organization? Your goal is to come up with something unique to your enterprise. You will learn how to apply this information in Chapter 8. See the Culture Czars CoreWorkflow below. Notice that we ended up adopting values-based language, even in our CoreWorkflow. We chose to represent the steps graphically because as we discussed earlier, according to Robert E. Horn, combining images with words is a powerful integration tool for groups and organizations.

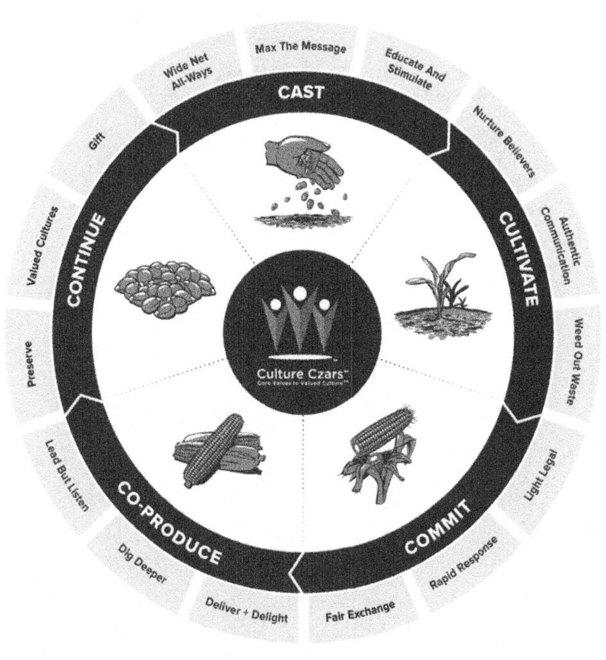

Culture Czars CoreWorkflow

CHAPTER 8

Deliver

To give my counsels all in one:
Your tuneful flame still careful fan;
Preserve the dignity of Man,
With soul erect;
And trust the Universal Plan
Will all protect.

—ROBERT BURNS, THE VISION

WHAT DOES A COMPANY look like when process, values, and purpose work harmoniously? What do projects look like? What does a single day in the life of the company look like? Until now, we have examined the cultural process from a collective point of view. Now that you have your people on board and your czars keeping everyone focused on core values, it's time for you to enjoy the many returns you will see from your investment. Using CoreVals to drive performance and happiness at work will free your time and eliminate many worries that distract you from the hands-on portion of the business—or what you really want to be doing with your work hours. How will you integrate culture into your days, weeks, months—and into the future? The key to driving your business is forming a continuum of culture.

How will you integrate culture into your days, weeks, months—and into the future? The key to driving your business is forming a continuum of culture.

Simon Sinek holds that applying consistent standards is crucial to maintaining trust. "It's like exercise, where consistency is more important than intensity. You can't go to the gym for nine hours and get in shape, but if you go for twenty minutes each day you'll see progress over time. If you're not seeing results, you're probably doing something wrong. Leadership is exactly the same way."[18] I would add that consistent leadership also builds trust, which is what makes companies thrive. Trust fosters innovation, accountability, and motivation to act for the greater good instead of personal gain. This mindset, in turn, creates trust with clients for even more benefits. For Culture Czars, a company's purpose acts as a blanket term for consistent forward movement around mission and motive. I call this the CorePurpose—the overarching company goal and reason for being.

Apply Consistently and Persistently

Having a clear starting point and well-defined idea of what success for the company looks like conveys clarity to employees and clients. Knowing why you are in business will lay the groundwork needed to list and articulate the values upon which all behavior in the company will be based.

---

18 Simon Sinek, "How Anyone Can Be the Leader They Wish They Had: An Interview with Simon Sinek," interview by Omaid Homayun, *Forbes*, June 1, 2016, https://www.forbes.com/sites/omaidhomayun/2016/06/01/how-anyone-can-be-the-leader-they-wish-they-had-interview-with-simon-sinek/#253a8faf2fca.

When I first introduced Lumiere's core values back in Chapter 1, I did not tell you that they were the building blocks for the company's overarching purpose. Let's look at them again, rooted as they are in purpose: *Believe, Connect, Teach & Learn, Have Fun.* Next we used a question and answer process (that we will discuss fully in a moment) to determine Lumiere's CorePurpose and came up with the following: *Generating 100,000 magic moments by 2020 and transforming forever the lives and achievements of our clients and their families.* Those four CoreVals are the fuel behind the company's vision—to generate 100,000 magic moments within this decade.

This isn't a guessing game, but one of context. Founder Kitsa and I articulated that vision based on what she achieves for her clients. Lumiere makes it possible for families to celebrate special moments big and small. These are the memory-makers that most families anticipate and strive for. They include—birthday parties, soccer and baseball games, trips to amusement parks, and play dates with friends. When therapy enables breakthroughs, Lumiere's clients are provided with new opportunities. These are the experiences that create magic moments. These are also the moments Kitsa and her team live for. We worked this vision into a three-year plan, broken down into annual segments, to propel Lumiere's culture and business into the future. The goal was a quantifiable, measurable purpose for what Kitsa and company wanted, with a clear understanding of who the beneficiaries would be.

If you feel you need help putting your CorePurpose together with the benefit of an outside perspective, you wouldn't be the first. This may be the same person who can provide objective interviews and assessments of your employees. Like surveys, direct interviews of your team members by an independent source can give you inside information straight from the floor and upper echelons alike.

Kitsa went this route, and she confides how refreshing this dynamic was for her. "When you are the founder of a company, it's important to be a part of the team. Your team doesn't want to hear you dictate. I appreciated an outside facilitator taking a fresh view because they're neutral and unbiased. Doing that put me in the audience instead of at the podium. I loved it, because then I really got to be on my team's side."

How to Construct the CorePurpose in Your Company

CEOs and leadership teams struggle with getting to a defined, measurable purpose for their business—one that speaks to the *why* and addresses all the components that I like to see and present to a team. Below is a questionnaire that can be applied to any enterprise that has been in business for at least a few years. Simply answer these questions to help define your CorePurpose:

First, Look Back

1. What have you done?
2. How many have you done?
3. Who have you done it for?

Next, Consider Where You Are Now

4. What are you doing now and for whom?

Then, Look to the Future

5. What will you do by (date, say, three years from now)?
6. Who will you do it for and how many?
7. Why will you do it?

The first three questions are reflective because they provide context and continuity to what you are doing now and where you are going next. Unless you have changed businesses or made a pivot, CEOs find it easier to determine their forward-looking purpose by beginning with where the company started. Numerically, it also makes the CorePurpose more exciting because the value of your company's future deliverable is higher by including what you have already produced. Also, because your company has grown, the scale of your future deliverable value is likely going to be significantly greater and this can really motivate you. Unless we pick a specific numeric goal to be achieved by a certain date, we will never know when we have achieved our purpose and our team will not be able to quantify the meaningful contributions they are eager to understand.

The last question, *why*, is the most important and yet it is one of the hardest concepts to decipher and put into words. You need to get introspective on why your customers, clients, or end users buy your product or service. Why do they buy what you sell and how does it benefit them? The *why* should be about them and not about you or your business. Even better, think about your value to your client's customer. Then you are aligned to your clients CorePurpose and have the same motives that they have, which will propel your conversations and your collective success.

During a workshop with Erin Diehl, Founder and CEO of improve it!, we dialogued about her company's CorePurpose using the question prompts listed above. When I asked her what she does, she responded, "We host improv training sessions for corporations." I followed up by asking why she does this. She answered, "To break down professionals' internal barriers. To get comfortable with the uncomfortable." To push her further, I asked "Why?" She answered simply, "Because it helps people grow." "How?" I inquired. "They become better version of themselves, professionally and personally." That's good, I thought. "So you do what you do at improve it! because it helps people become better versions of themselves?" She nodded enthusiastically, and we agreed that this was a much more compelling answer than her original one.

The rest of our conversation focused on quantifiable measures. I asked her how long she had been helping people become better versions of themselves. She explained that in the four years of her business, she had trained about 12,500. I asked her to share with me what she was doing currently, and she described how she averaged twenty-five to thirty-five people per workshop and sometimes had one hundred people or more in attendance. For 2018, improve it! planned to host more than eighty workshops using six lead facilitators and twelve co-facilitators to train about four thousand people. Using those numbers as estimates, we calculated they would train approximately thirty-thousand people by 2021.

Through this conversation, we arrived at her company's CorePurpose: *By 2021, improve it! will have trained thirty-thousand people in our live improv training sessions so that they can become better versions of themselves and keep growing personally and professionally.* Imagine how her trainers feel once they realize they are helping people become better versions of themselves as opposed to "hosting improv training sessions for corporations." She reports her trainers now feel more motivated around the purpose of the organization and the impact that they are making on the world.

In another recent CorePurpose consult with Lisa Scott, immigration attorney of Scott Global Migration Law Group, I used the same question format. "Why do you do what you do?" I asked. "So that my clients can get immigration visas," she said. "But that's a what, not a why," I pressed. "Okay, so that I can help them build better lives," she responded. "But why? Keep going," I encouraged. "So that we keep families together—yes that's it! That's our why. We do what we do to keep families together," Lisa exclaimed. This might be good enough and is certainly more emotive and purposeful than securing visas, but could we go further? Why do families want to stay together? Is it to ensure they can feel safe being close to loved ones or can survive by pooling resources? The point is to keep peeling back the layers of your purpose and to find the essence of the value you provide. If you arrive at something that stirs emotions, you know you have a purpose that is meaningful and that people can get behind.

SABRE saw similar results during our CorePurpose consults. Using the exercise above, David Nance and his management team determined that their CorePurpose was *To provide protection and safety to seventy million heroes by 2021.* This exciting number was determined by combining all the personal safety products that SABRE had shipped since their inception with their projections through 2021. We educated their workers to believe that they weren't just selling pepper spray, with a focus on the number of boxes shipped. They were helping to protect people and save lives with the best-quality pepper spray on the market, while also providing the least lethal option available to law enforcement.

Sometimes arriving at a CorePurpose is not a linear process, as was the case with the digital marketing agency Matchnode. The founders knew from the beginning that their goal was to help small business owners, and since that purpose resonated with them, they never questioned it. They started to notice relatively quickly, however, that their best clients were also some of their biggest clients, including major Chicago sporting franchises who loved the results that Matchnode was delivering. They were happy to build a more solid financial footing for their business, but they were aware that the realities of their business didn't match with their CorePurpose.

Matchnode is an analytical agency, centered on conversions—actions people take on the other side of an ad, like buying concert tickets or signing up to refinance a home. This aspect is what differentiates the company and allows them to calculate how many conversions they drive for clients. When I consulted with the leadership team, we realized that Matchnode's focus on the people on the *other side* of the ad—their clients' customers—was their motivating factor. The purpose was to give people access to experiences. "When we made this connection, there was a palpable shift in the room," said co-founder Brian Davidson.

We looked back at the start of the business in 2013 and counted all of their clients, how many conversions they drove, and how many lives they improved. Ultimately, they were improving several hundred thousand lives a year. After more discussion and calculations, we arrived at Matchnode's CorePurpose: *To improve two million lives by October 10, 2020.*

Brian's co-founder Chris Madden is the first to admit that uncovering Matchnode's CorePurpose required intentional work spent on defining its core values and defining its culture:

> We were more prepared to find our [CorePurpose] breakthrough because we had been doing a lot of groundwork with our core values. We keenly focused on them and refined them. When we arrived at our purpose, the mood of the conversation did change in the way that was really clear to us. But we had to do the foundational work first.

When Matchnode's leaders identified their CorePurpose, they were able to lead a culture, not just a company because they were extending their values downstream to their customers as well as internally to their team. Being able to look to the past, present, and future and identify quantifiable measures was meaningful for the operation and provided a powerful context to the work they do.

A great culture is only complete when its CorePurpose is in place. Only then will people know what the company is about in big-picture terms, where they fit, and how to operate. It makes employees feel valued and like they are making meaningful contributions to the world, not just showing up to work because they have to. It might sound obvious, but people care about how they feel, and they want to feel real.

Images help us keep information simple, yet clearly stated. Everyone connects swiftly and strongly to visual aids. The communication power of road signs, photographs, and infographics works well in a busy, hurried world. How do you take 9 Deeds and boil them down to something simple? By using an infographic called the CoreChart.

The CoreChart combines your CorePurpose, CoreVals, and CoreWorkflow into a visual representation that illustrates:

- What you do, where, and how
- Who you do it for
- By when and why

The CoreChart illuminates the values that you will put in your hearts and on your walls. Though I have shown examples of all processes throughout the book, when it comes to CoreCharts most companies and organizations feel they are confidential and too closely tied to their competitive advantages. For this reason, I will only share a few that I have been granted permission to use.

As you can see, SABRE's CoreChart succinctly addresses the *who, what, why, when, where,* and *how many*, to equal the CorePurpose; the CoreWorkflow and CoreVals together address the *how we will do it* question. Why does this matter? Who cares? Your people do. If they do, your customers will too. If they do, your business will flourish, and so will you. CoreChart posters are the result of rigorous discovery, discernment, and description. They reach out to readers, clients, customers, employees, executives, and say, "Hey, here's what we're all about." They break down the wall between the company and everyone else. They make the beliefs of the people who work there transparent and full of color.

Matchnode was able to creatively incorporate their logo for an effective visual. Furthermore, depending on the circumstances, they can choose to include the detailed CoreChart descriptors or just use the simple chart.

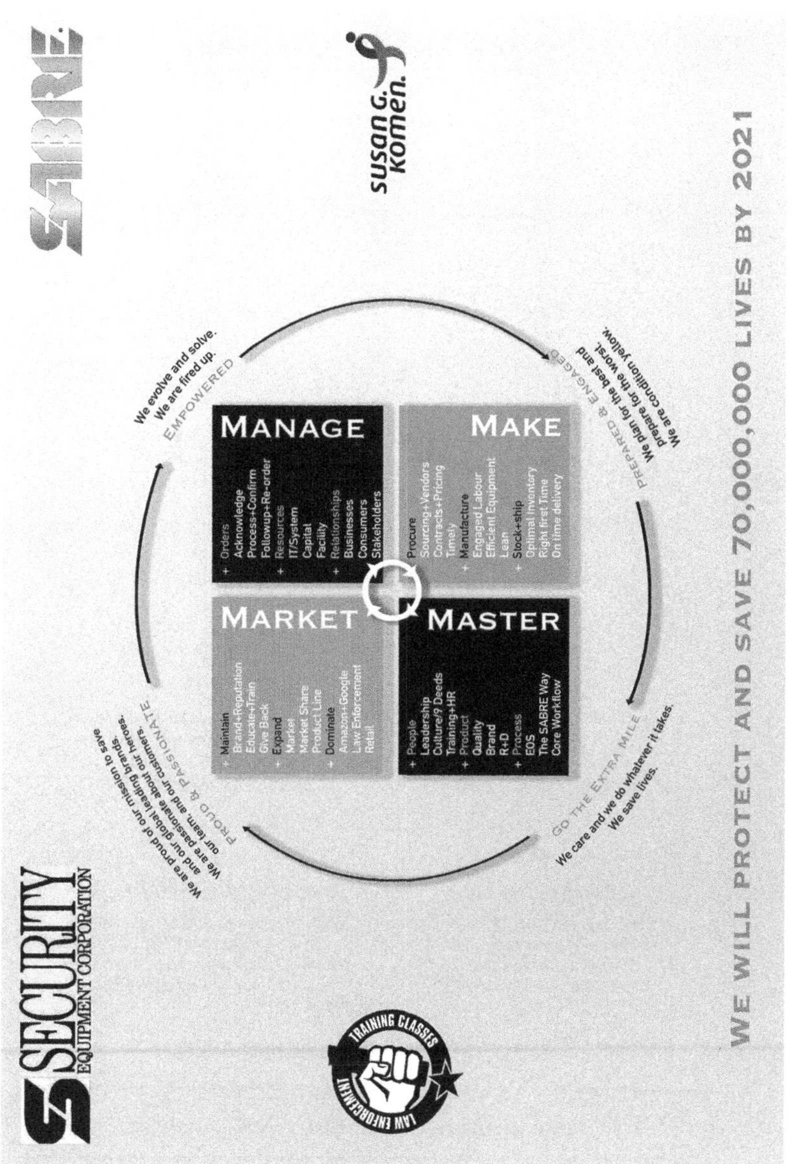

SABRE's CoreChart

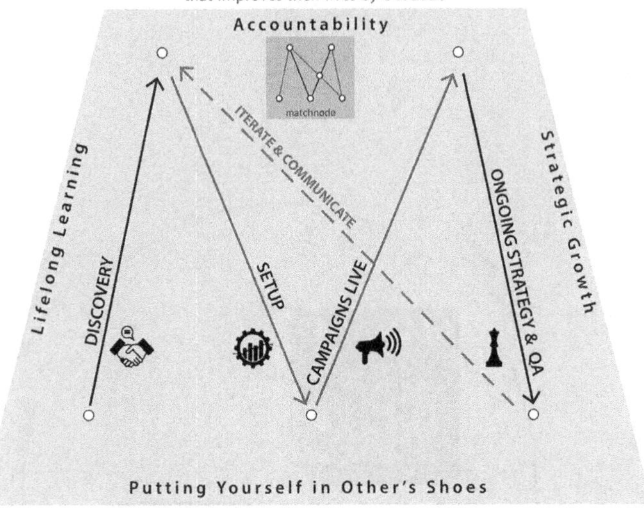

DISCOVERY

- Intro & Analytics Review
- Present SOW
- Commence 90 day sprint
- New relationship interview

SETUP

- Access, invoice, creative, approval, Trello & Slack
- Kickoff call: define success, KPIs, budget, plan
- 18 step campaign checklist
- Weekly 30 minute call

CAMPAIGNS LIVE

- Leverage custom software for decision support
- Weekly calls, KPIs & strategy, make plan
- Execute next test campaign
- Iterative cycle improvements

ONGOING STRATEGY & QA

- Consistent communication & regular testing
- "Fresh eyes" meetings & NPS feedback
- Review work, strategy, and next steps per SOW
- Seasonal, quarterly, annual planning

Matchnode CoreChart

 To review in more detail, visit www.cultureczars.com

The CoreChart will allow all of your stakeholders to attach meaning to their work—to know where they fit in the process and how to go about their work in an effective, team-oriented manner. Because it is quantifiable and date-stamped, they know when they will get there. Dictate your core values address in front of the CoreChart and it becomes a powerful communication tool. It tells your customers what to expect when they work with you and tells your vendors how to align with you.

Let's say you've got your CoreVals in words and on walls. You've got a CoreChart, and your business life looks rosy. As ancient Chinese philosophers warned in the *I Ching,* or the "Book of Changes," this can be a dangerous situation. When you are riding high on success, it's tempting to rest on those laurels and take it easy for a while. At this stage of core value maintenance, breakdown can occur—after the focus groups and surveys and system implementations, when passion for culture cools. If you focus on applying processes consistently and persistently, the culture continues on a positive trend. If not, it will devolve.

To prevent regression, simply keep in mind the dysfunctional aspects of business that good culture has helped you avoid, reduce, or purge:

- Negative employees
- Difficult conversation avoidance
- Fear of conflict
- Lack of trust
- Avoidance of accountability
- Disregard for team objectives
- Sexual harassment or other anti-social behaviors

Also, remember positive attributes that have improved or increased:

- Morale
- Teamwork
- Motivation
- Commitment
- Goal achievement
- Performance

Tasks should be locked into your calendar to ensure monitoring your culture will happen like clockwork, without a second thought. When it comes time to make decisions, you'll look to your CoreChart and spend less time agonizing or procrastinating, and more time doing the right thing.

Thoughts from a Culture Czar

"*The fact is, all your employees know where the problems lie. They know the people they'd rather not work with. Yet, they just sort of accept it, and they keep doing their job. But I don't want to have a company that way. I don't want people to accept mediocrity. I don't want people to accept bad conditions. I want them to come to work wanting to be there. I want them to participate in our growth. Some of our change has also been about whether you're in line with the fact that we are trying to grow as a company. I say you either want to be a part of our growth, or you go. So, it's grow or go.*"

—DEE ROBINSON,
FOUNDER AND CEO OF ROBINSON HILL

EXERCISE 8: DELIVER

A. Construe your CorePurpose. Follow the examples in this chapter to define your company purpose. Consult with your team and work through the seven questions, but also do some quiet contemplation on your own. The purpose of the business generally evolves from the CEO's vision for what they want the company to achieve over time. Quantify it and date-stamp it to determine how much and by when. State who you will do it for (your clients, customers, etc.), and most importantly, understand and describe why you will do it. This becomes your CorePurpose, your reason for being. See the example below for Culture Czars CorePurpose:

> Culture Czar's CorePurpose: *To create 2020 Culture Czars by 2020 and deliver $1 billion in value globally through helping 100,000 employees love where they work and why they work, so that they are fulfilled, loyal, and engaged.*

First, Look Back

1. What have you done?

____

____

2. How many have you done?

____

____

3. Who have you done it for?

Next, Consider Where You Are Now

4. What are you doing now and for whom?

Then, Look to the Future

5. What will you do by (date, say, three years from now)?

6. Who will you do it for and how many?

7. Why will you do it?

Consider how you will measure progress toward your goal. For example, Lumiere has a counter that literally gets hit every time a client has a magic moment. A numeric read-out is visible for all to see, and it is thrilling to watch the magic moments occur and the counter climb toward the goal of 100,000. In addition, a photo of the child's experience is often taken and shared with the parent, or posted to social media.

B. Draft your CoreChart. Bring your CorePurpose together with your CoreWorkflow from Chapter 7, and your CoreVals from Chapter 3, to draft your CoreChart. Continue the theme and look at what you established earlier. See the image below for an example of Culture Czars' CoreChart.

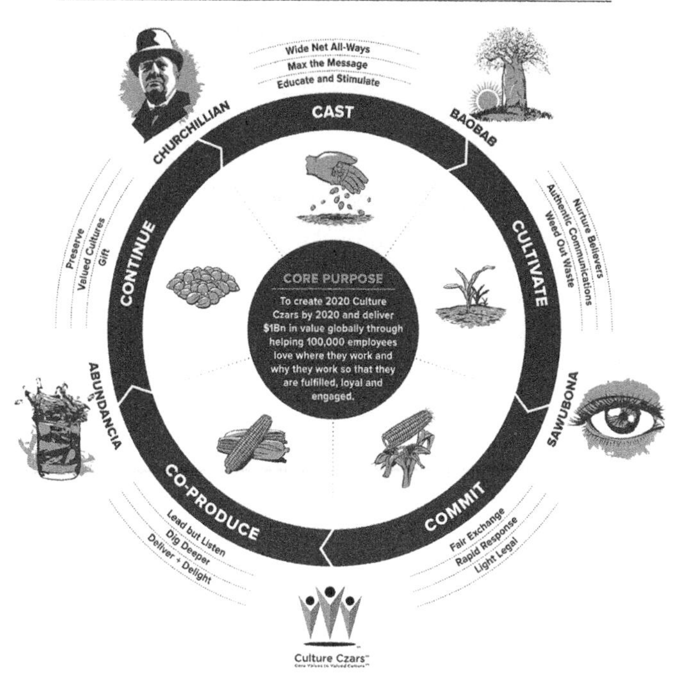

Culture Czars CoreChart

This variation on our CoreChart is labeled to show how it addresses all the strategic questions of an organization in one succinct diagram. Do all of your employees and stakeholders have the answers to these questions in any kind of visible and memorable one-page document today? This is what is so appealing about the CoreChart.

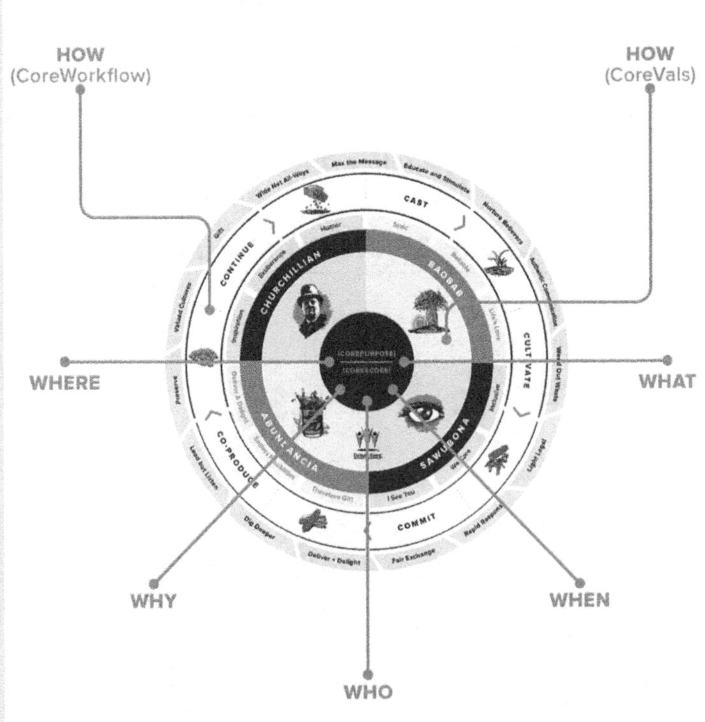

Culture Czars CoreChart with labels showing how the chart addresses all the strategic questions

CHAPTER 9

Determine

I saw your pulse's maddening play,
Wild-send you Pleasure's devious way,
Misled by Fancy's meteor-ray,
By passion driven;
But yet the light that led astray
Was light from Heaven.

—ROBERT BURNS, THE VISION

PART OF THE PURPOSE of measuring the condition of your culture is to follow the return on your investment (ROI). When you picked up this book, your natural curiosity about, or attraction to building culture was probably offset by what you would have to invest. *How much time/money/effort is this going to take?* You are now getting a clearer picture of the extent of your contribution. You are also getting a sense of the exponential dividends you will receive. You may have already acquired some hard-earned peace of mind.

Just the anticipation of better focus, more time, and less worry for yourself may be worth the effort. Then factor in greater employee engagement, increased productivity and innovation, and an improved image with your customers, and you begin to see where increased satisfaction meets higher revenues. Don't fret over the intangible rewards—embrace them. They lead to real, measurable improvement.

You will use a variety of tools to measure the quality and quantity of the benefits that flow from your culture quest. These include:

- Goal achievement reports
- Financial reports
- Employee evaluations
- Quarterly and annual surveys
- Consultant interviews
- Spontaneous testing
- Gut checks

First, I'll show you the money. You'll get the quantitative measurements that will tell you how far your culture has driven your business month by month. Next, I'll show you how to become more in tune with changes in office relations, productivity, and core value applications, to ensure your intuitive radar will always be on.

Measure Quantity and Quality

You'll find new insights into your CoreScore by comparing its ups and downs with your company's metrics on meeting performance objectives and revenue goals. You probably already measure those things, not just because it reveals the health of your business, but because it provides benchmarks for employees. Setting clear goals backed up by data tells people how to go about their jobs and puts everyone on the same scale of accountability.

What is your method for measuring performance and holding the right people accountable? If you use an operating system like Agile, you likely set short- and long-term goals on a departmental and project basis. The path toward accomplishment is marked by the specific tasks required and the level of achievement desired. These goals are the things that absolutely must be done, with a timeline and expectations. Agile calls them "key performance indicators" (KPIs). When individuals and teams handle these indicators as planned, they focus well and get projects done on time with an acceptable—or higher—level of competence.

Whichever operating system you use, be sure to track performance milestones in each role or department. This is one more way to communicate to your team what is expected of them. Measuring those KPIs makes it easier for employees to understand your goals—and for you to know they understand them. Then there's no room for prevarication or excuses. Everyone's on the same path, moving forward. Kitsa Antonopoulos points out that this type of measurement shows when either an individual or an established workflow underperforms: "If something falls off in a metric, we dig around and poke, poke, poke to find where we missed something. Then it's easy for us to course-correct, make adjustments, or whatever we need to do."

These are all things that feed the culture, to ensure it drives your business toward success. You might want to create your own metric that tracks your workplace culture alongside your market performance. David Nance reports that SABRE's CoreScore and financials indicate his 9 Deeds investment has done just that: "Top-line sales are up double digits. That requires production people to do a lot more. You have to get a lot more product out the door, and you're not going to keep customers if you're not filling their orders.

We're more efficient in manufacturing and shipping because morale has gone from okay to good. And we're still improving."

David also notes some things are easier to measure than others. That implies some are more difficult, and he means culture and the "softer" side of business. That won't stop us from trying to successfully get there. Why are issues related to human resources called the "soft" side of business anyway? They certainly pack a punch when it comes to the bottom line. The term *soft* really means the side of business that is less easily quantified. The quality of people's work experience does indeed come down to dollars and cents. If the culture is rocking, people stay in their jobs and do them well. That's less money spent on recruitment and severance, and potentially more money coming in, if the market is responsive. This is why gathering data on the condition of your culture is worthwhile. Just as Kitsa will pursue a fall-off in measurable performance, you can follow up on dips in overall cultural health. The data will show you where to target your efforts.

One measurement that you probably already use is the employee annual evaluation. You may use it to determine pay grade, bonus eligibility, and promotions, as well as redirections and terminations. You might also receive open-ended feedback from employees on all kinds of topics, and can take the opportunity to build interpersonal rapport. Now, add cultural markers to your evaluation structure. It won't cost you more, and it will give you one additional way to measure culture. Include CoreScore information in the annual, biannual, or quarterly evaluation and in the employee's file.

A more objective way to get employee feedback is through surveys. These are easy to administer and tally for results. You can use an online program or put together your own email or print questionnaires. Asking each of your team members the same questions will give you a range of responses, which you can then rank numerically and average. I suggest a core list of evergreen questions, plus some relating to the company's current situation.

See www.cultureczars.com/the-culture-fix-book for *The Culture Fix* Employee Poll, a free online questionnaire.

How do you compose your questionnaire? First, get some baseline information on the respondent's role, rank within the company, and length of service. Then move on to how *they* would rate the culture. Or, if you would prefer to use a standard set of questions, use *The Culture Fix* Employee Poll below.

The Culture Fix Employee Poll

1. How would you describe the company's culture today?
2. If the company was a person, what kind of person would it be?
3. What value or behavior would you like to see more of?
4. Which of the company's core values can you state from memory?
5. The company's stated values are __________. Do you feel that these accurately portray the organization and how we work together? Why or why not?
6. Name one or two of your coworkers who best embody those values and why.

Repeating this type of survey quarterly or annually will demonstrate trends. Some employers go even further. As he shares in his book, *The Power of Company Culture,* business executive Chris Dyer surveys his employees weekly. He uses a super-quick, open-ended, one-question survey to query his staff on the pressing issue of the moment. He alternates with a weekly pulse of more general questions about the work experience, such as: *What do we do well? What is your biggest obstacle? How could we help our clients more?* This gives Dyer fifty-two chances to get qualitative data that he might otherwise never have compiled. Part of the time, he shares the survey results with everybody. He can then ask follow-up questions about that information, if he chooses. More importantly, the tactic directly benefits the culture. "People learn more about their coworkers and feel connected when others share their views," he writes. "Overall, this helps them be on the same page. Sharing also appears to spur conversations among team members toward solving problems, without any prompting by senior management."[19] That effect, CEOs will agree, is priceless.

If you want to free up your people to be as honest as possible and get some truly in-depth interviews, this is the way to go. Clearly, sitting Employee X down and interviewing him yourself is not the most objective tactic. Choose an external consultant to speak with your employees once a year. Again, you can use what you learn to add to your company's CoreScore. If core values are guiding behavior and decision making—or if they are not—you'll find out.

Finally, two more casual ways of gathering data will help give you the big picture on your organization's culture: one

19 Chris Dyer, *The Power of Company Culture* (London: Kogan Page Limited, 2018), 84.

comes from your staff and the other from yourself. Remember my daughter, Chloe? Although she didn't work at Lextech, during time spent hanging out with me, she had absorbed the five core values that made its culture great. On some level, just knowing that people are aware of them and can repeat them tells you all you need to know. I advocate spontaneous testing in that regard. You can and should talk to your staff outside of meetings and formal occasions. Stop them in the hallway, ask how things are going, and then ask them to recite the core values. Or have them quiz you! Whatever the answers, focus on the positive. Then, making notes back at your desk, record the level of success. Plot the numbers on a graph or find another way to track the success rate over time. Each of these methods for gathering data can be given a numeric score, just like the CoreScore. You may keep them separate or pour them all into one grand spreadsheet. Then you can cross-analyze specific elements.

There is one last measurement that you can't outsource: the gut check. As Julie Mitchell, founder of Torq Ride, shared with me:

> One thing with culture is that once you get it right, you don't really need to change the values. As you go through that process, it takes some time. It's not an exercise that you can do in a couple of hours. You need to test this stuff out. I think that it's fair that when you get it right, you don't need to change it, but it's okay to get it wrong. It's okay to identify what the values are and then revisit it and shape it...until you get into a place where it just feels like it's real, authentic, actionable, and universally embraced.

Pick a time to ask yourself each week how *you* feel the culture is doing. Maybe it's when you walk in the door on Mondays or leave on Fridays, or after a scheduled weekly meeting. Create your own scale of one to five and define what those increments mean. As Julie points out, it's okay to make some revisions if you intuitively feel like things aren't right. Continue your regular gut checks until it feels right. Then, once a week, define the health of your culture. Does it feel real?

A Final Word about ROI

Building culture is the lowest investment/highest return initiative you can bring to your company. Implementing a cultural plan is less expensive, less risky, and more personally rewarding than venturing into new markets, new products, the next marketing campaign, or the next acquisition that your partner or shareholders want. For a few thousand dollars and some team time, you will get infinite intangible benefits and an ROI—or ROC (Return on Culture)—that will certainly be one of your best investments.

I'll remind you now of my own purpose, when it comes to culture: my hope is that companies all over the world will shift toward valuing culture and improving the lives of people who work—in enterprises of all kinds.

I'll remind you now of my own purpose, when it comes to culture: my hope is that companies all over the world will shift toward valuing culture and improving the lives of people who work—in enterprises of all kinds. In this book's introduction, I asked you to imagine how much greater the worldwide level of happiness would be if people did this. Let me add to that the trickledown benefit. With a global emphasis on workplace culture, how prosperous could our world be? Given the boost in money-generating performance, the value of the world economy might see an uptick of five percent, ten percent, or more! People who are happy at work are more productive. Associates who feel valued and sense that they are making a meaningful contributions to the world will give you more and stay with you longer.

If you've still got your feet on the ground, consider how your own motivation for getting out of bed in the morning could improve. Meaghan Mullgardt of SABRE perfectly describes how working on culture revolutionized her own outlook, "I'm a lot more excited to come to work these days—and I'm part of the family that owns the company. I didn't always feel passionate about it, but I do now."

Talk about a return on investment! I personally wish to create at least 2,020 Culture Czars by 2020. In financial terms, if we can lift the revenues of 2,020 small businesses with, say ten million dollars in revenue, by just five percent, we can create a one billion dollar impact on the business community in a single year. Once those businesses are doing twenty million dollars in revenue, we can have twice the impact. If this is the return, what has been the cost, and what is the ROC? What has implementing these 9 Deeds in your company cost you? Some time, for sure, yet mostly internal resources that the business was already carrying—the value of your time and that of your Culture Czars. Other costs may include some copies of *The Culture Fix* and related books, plus some printing and promotional products. Generally speaking, nothing huge. Let's calculate a possible ROC.

Formula for Calculating ROC after implementing *The Culture Fix:*

$$\frac{\text{Increase in Profits (Total Return)} - \text{Total Cost}}{\text{Team time} + \text{Printing costs} + \text{Event costs} + \text{Other costs (Total Cost)}} \times 100 = \%\ \text{(ROC)}$$

Here's a simple explanation. For a $10 million company achieving a 10 percent net profit, that is able to credit *The Culture Fix* with even a 10 percent lift in profits in the first year, then the numerator is $100,000. Let's say that the company spent a total of ten man-hours per week, over nine weeks, at an assumed internal cost of $50 per hour. Then, the team time cost is approximately $4,500. For easy math, let's say that another $5,500 was spent on printing, giveaways, T-shirts, and some event costs, for a total numerator cost of $10,000. This results in a 10x return or, using the formula above, a 900% Return on Culture. Most companies I know that have implemented this or similar programs would easily accept that they have netted a 10x return, or more. And most would credit the project with yielding a much higher profit lift than 10 percent.

What about the ROC for your company? What do you think working on your culture has been worth? What will the uptick in revenues be, and what will the impact on the bottom line be?

Use the ROC calculator at www.cultureczars.com/the-culture-fix-book to calculate your return on investment, and then share your results with me via email to Will@CultureCzars.com.

What is the risk of implementing these 9 Deeds in 90 Days? It's pretty low, isn't it? You really have very little to lose and so much to gain from bringing your core values alive, making them thrive, and using them to drive your organization. As stated in the beginning of the book, there is no other initiative an executive can undertake that:

- Requires a low capital investment
- Produces the highest return
- Is one of the most rewarding experiences you can have alongside your team

Your quality and quantity assessments are your tools for keeping your finger on the pulse of your company's culture. More data gives you a richer picture of the complex workplace dynamic that is culture. Identifying measurable results will give direction on how to proceed, based on what is working in your culture. This will show you how to drive culture so that it drives your business. When everything is moving in synchronicity, you will notice improvements in team and company performance. Once you add up the numbers, you'll be able to see how well your cultural efforts drive your business toward success.

Few elements of doing business are more important than a culture that includes top people performing to their full potential, in a tight team that is meeting or exceeding its goals—and having fun doing it! In addition to creating an atmosphere where you want to go to work every day, great culture is your greatest business asset. Get it right, and success will follow.

Thoughts from a Culture Czar

We're always fighting culture on two fronts—how we manage ourselves internally as a business, and then how we look in the public eye and how we interact with our customers.... I think when the culture goes to hell it's not just hard, it's emotionally distressing....I have no question this business would be bankrupt financially if we didn't have the culture that we do. So it's easy to brush over a lot of this if your top line is great. Sales solve all... for a while it does, but as you grow and scale, the business becomes at the mercy of whatever the manager thinks it should be for their department, and maybe that'll work and maybe it won't, but...I don't think we would have pulled this business back from the brink without the culture that we have. Going forward from that, culture leads to sales here...it leads to repeat customers. It leads to staff who hang out together on the weekends when they're not working. All of that translates into sales, because people come in and they buy and have a good time.

–BRIAN WASPI,
CEO OF CLEAR WATER OUTDOOR

EXERCISE 9: DETERMINE

Numbers will tell you what type of returns your investment in culture is generating—both for your revenues and for the well-being of your employees. Collect data and score the culture to determine your ROC.

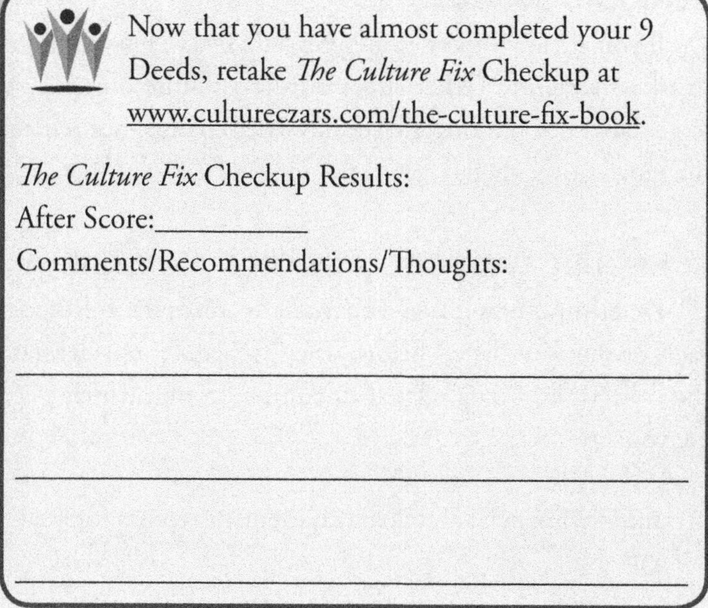

Now that you have almost completed your 9 Deeds, retake *The Culture Fix* Checkup at www.cultureczars.com/the-culture-fix-book.

The Culture Fix Checkup Results:
After Score:__________
Comments/Recommendations/Thoughts:

____

____

____

A. Keep records. You will want to create your own records for the metrics discussed in this chapter. Set up a system related to culture that includes:

- A calendar
- Copies of financial reports
- Departmental performance statistics
- Employee CoreScores
- Survey templates
- Survey results

B. Build in the following cultural measurements:

EMPLOYEE ANNUAL EVALUATIONS

Add employees' CoreScores to their files and discuss core values during evaluative meetings. Create one or more baseline questions about culture to ask every employee at evaluation time.

PERIODIC SURVEYS

If you already survey employees, add five to ten questions to ask consistently. Otherwise, institute a culture-only survey to get baseline opinions and see how they change—or remain the same—over time.

SCHEDULE DATA COLLECTION & ANALYSIS

Determine how often you want to measure culture in each of the ways listed below. Then, schedule and delegate the collection of data related to culture, noting which steps are yours to take:

1. Import financial and goal achievement reports for analysis.

____

____

2. Compile CoreScores and survey question results from employee annual evaluations.

____

____

3. Keep count of the number of monthly award nominations received.

___

___

4. Facilitate consultant interviews of staff and compile results.

___

___

5. Do spontaneous testing of team members and record results.

___

___

6. Perform gut checks on how real the culture feels.

___

___

Conclusion

Begins and Ends with Culture

NOW THAT YOU HAVE completed *The Culture Fix*, you are ready to take your company culture to new places. Throughout this process, you have learned how to implement 9 Deeds in 90 Days to create an aligned, valued culture where:

- Everyone is accountable, on the same page, and pulling together
- Teams make decisions the same way that leadership would
- Difficult conversations that promote healthy, safe relationships are embraced, not avoided
- The right people are hired and retained, and the cultural misfits are respectfully unhired
- Measurable and significant increases in sales and profits are credited to the culture

Whether you are a novice leader or a seasoned one, infusing culture into your business can create phenomenal rewards for yourself and your team. As Linda Maclachlan, CEO of Entara shared with me:

> When you start your own company…nobody ever promotes you. I was CEO of a company of a couple people. Now we've got sixty here, but

> I still hold the same title. What has changed is my understanding of leadership and of the things that matter and the things that have the best return. [It's] not even close to where I was…fifteen years ago. And [culture] is a perfect example. I think that the return on doing core values work is huge.

By reading this book and implementing these tactics in your life and your company/organization, you've joined our growing community of Culture Czars to become a champion of corporate culture. What you do in connection with company culture will be yours to own, and its expression will naturally develop from your personal style. You'll find a way that's right for you.

You now know that you are not just a leader of a company, you are the leader of a culture—a much more grandiose and fulfilling leadership role with a greater mission and purpose. However, even the most dynamic boss can't propagate culture alone, so you need champions who get it. These "czars" of culture will help you bring every team member on board and monitor the company's cultural health. Your czars may include upper management colleagues, department heads, HR gurus, or any employees who display passion for cultural direction. You may even choose to bring in a consultant to facilitate the process. You are still at the top, and now that you have finished the program, you are the Culture Czar in your company.

Most people work, but how many people love *where* they work and *why* they work? We can create multiple billion dollars of value on a global basis by helping organizations thrive in truly valued cultures where employees are valued and feel that they are doing something meaningful. There is no greater journey that a CEO or entrepreneur can embark on than enhancing their organizational culture. It requires the lowest investment, yields the highest return, and is fun and rewarding for everyone involved. Many companies have core values on the wall, but have not created a valued culture where people thrive and are the best that they can be.

At Culture Czars, we help organizations go from simply having core values to truly having a valued culture. We guide them toward bringing their culture alive and making it thrive. This is achieved when employees, associates, and stakeholders feel valued and believe they are making meaningful contributions every day. Turning core values into a valued culture means going from simply having a core values poster on the wall to having core values embodied in each decision and strategy. With this as the foundation, employees and CEOs can love *where* they work (Culture) and love *why* they work (CorePurpose).

When you lead a team with your core values as a compass, you are contributing to a new style of leadership that is less about strength and assertiveness, and more about inclusion, connection, and authenticity. As the Zulu greeting, *sawubona* reminds us, every moment is an opportunity for meaningful connection—if we use it that way. Connection benefits everyone. Authentic interactions are more likely to leave people feeling that they're working at the right place—with the right people. One possible response to *sawubona* is, *"Yebo, sawubona,"* which means, "I see you seeing me." This verbal exchange shows how humans can create connection cycles. When I feel seen, I'm more likely to see you. *Really* see you. I can see the value that you bring to my day, my work, my life. In turn, I know that you appreciate my value and authenticity.

From the time I was a child in Zambia building forts for my friends, my major impetus has been inclusion. I have always had the desire and the need to include people. Ultimately, this is what a corporate culture can do for a workplace. It's not just about making the work environment more enriching, it's also about making each and every individual feel like they belong to something bigger than themselves.

When an individual feels included, this creates community. Outside of all of the quantifiable returns we've discussed within these pages, imagine the benefits of creating this sense of community for the people on your team. I believe *The Culture Fix* is for all teams, including not-for-profits, charitable and religious organizations, and political organizations. Having seen the transformations that a valued culture can bring to workplaces and organizations, many people implement the same changes in their own homes. They become more present in their decision making and life choices, exemplifying for the next generation that leading with your core values creates profound transformations. The person's home, community, and world become more inclusive, welcoming, and peaceful environments for themselves and the people around them. Can there be any greater reward?

Having completed 9 Deeds in 90 Days, you have completed the Culture Czars program and now hold the key to *The Culture Fix*. Kick open the door to a deeper meaning in your work and a tighter connection to the people with whom you spend your work days. It begins and ends with you, the leader, the Culture Czar.

Endnotes

1. Gallup, "State of the American Workplace," 2017.
2. Bradford, William C., Reaching the Visual Learner: Teaching Property Through Art (September 1, 2011). The Law Teacher Vol. 11, 2004. Available at SSRN: https://ssrn.com/abstract=587201
3. Robert E. Horn, "Visual Language and Converging Technologies in the Next 10-15 Years (and Beyond)" (Paper presented at the National Science Foundation Conference on Converging Technologies for Improving Human Performance, Dec. 3-4, 2001).
4. Mercer, "Mercer Global Talent Trends 2018 Study," https://www.mercer.com/our-thinking/career/global-talent-hr-trends.html#.
5. *How Southwest Airlines built its culture*, YouTube video, 5:35, posted by World of Business Ideas, October 20, 2016, https://www.youtube.com/watch?v=8_CeFiUkV7s&feature=youtu.be.
6. *Start with Why*, YouTube video, 18:01, posted by TEDx Talks, September 28, 2009, https://www.youtube.com/watch?time_continue=2&v=u4ZoJKF_VuA.
7. John G. Stumpf. "The Vision & Values of Wells Fargo." Accessed January 28, 2019. http://www.damicofcg.com/files/74720/Vision%20%26%20Values.pdf.
8. Daniel Pink, Drive: *The Surprising Truth About What Motivates Us* (New York: Penguin Press, 2009), 71.
9. Daniel Coyle, *The Culture Code: The Secrets of Highly Successful Groups* (New York: Random House, 2018), 6.
10. Steve Jobs Marketing Strategy, YouTube video, 6:58, posted by "Inspiring Videos," February 28, 2015, https://www.youtube.com/watch?v=mMBQwAe45jc.

11. *Steve Jobs talks About Core Values at D8 2010*, YouTube video, 2:28, posted by "SteveNote," January 5, 2012, https://www.youtube.com/watch?v=5mKxekNhMqY&feature=youtu.be.

12. Adam Lashinsky, "The Cook Doctrine at Apple," *Fortune*, January 22, 2009, http://fortune.com/2009/01/22/the-cook-doctrine-at-apple/.

13. Simon Sinek, *Find Your Why: A Practical Guide to Discovering Purpose for You or Your Team* (New York: Penguin Press, 2017), 16.

14. James Kerr, "Uber: What Happened to Your Core Values," *Inc. Magazine*, December 4, 2017, https://www.inc.com/james-kerr/uber-what-happened-to-your-core-values.html.

15. Daniel Coyle, *The Culture Code: The Secrets of Highly Successful Groups* (New York: Random House, 2018), 107.

16. Simon Sinek, *Start With Why: How Great Leaders Inspire Everyone to Take Action* (New York: Penguin Press, 2009), 85.

17. Geoff Smart and Randy Street, *Who* (New York: Random House, 2008).

18. Simon Sinek, "How Anyone Can Be the Leader They Wish They Had: An Interview with Simon Sinek," interview by Omaid Homayun, *Forbes*, June 1, 2016, https://www.forbes.com/sites/omaidhomayun/2016/06/01/how-anyone-can-be-the-leader-they-wish-they-had-interview-with-simon-sinek/#253a8faf2fca.

19. Chris Dyer, *The Power of Company Culture* (London: Kogan Page Limited, 2018), 84.

Products and Services

Culture Czars is for you if you find yourself thinking: "My employees don't seem to care," "I can't attract the best employees," "I can't keep my best employees," "My employees aren't accountable," "I don't love the feeling of walking into my own office," "We spend too much time talking about this problematic employee," "There is too much drama and negative talk in the workplace," "It seems like I have to make all of the decisions," or "I don't know how to start and satisfactorily finish a difficult conversation."

Through speaking events, workshops, subscriptions, and a variety of implementations, Will Scott can help you enhance your culture and help your team work more effectively together!

Speaking

Hire Culture Czar, Will Scott to speak at your next event! Through an interactive session with live demos, customized formats and durations to fit your organization's needs, an overview of the 9 Deeds in 90 Days, and a free copy of The Culture Fix, Will encourages your team to love where they work, and why they work.

Subscription

With a monthly subscription to Culture Czars, you get one-on-one coaching, workbooks/training materials, live members-only webinars, a free copy of The Culture Fix, and an online library full of recorded webinars and training videos (3-month minimum subscription is recommended).

Workshops

Will Scott offers several full- and partial-day facilitated workshops to include illustrative companion workbooks, tips and tools, and a copy of The Culture Fix. Workshop 1 is on discerning your core values; Workshop 2 is about building a valued culture. Buy 2 seats and bring your whole team!

Implementation

Will Scott offers a culture-health audit and assessment, staff surveys and interviews, discovery workshops, employee evaluations, leadership team facilitation, Culture Czar training, valued culture implementation, on-site guidance and success commitment, and a free copy of The Culture Fix with each service. No matter what you are looking for, Will has the resources and support you need to make the culture change you're looking for!

Culture Czars Academy

For a low monthly subscription to The Culture Czars Academy, you can access video training and all the tools you need in order to implement a successful culture fix program in your company or for a client. Just go to www.cultureczars.academy now to subscribe and begin bringing cultures *Alive* and make them *Thrive* so they *Drive* performance. Email Will@CultureCzars to get $100 off your first month!

Additional Resources

To access additional resources—including The Culture Fix Workbook, subscribe to Culture Czars at https://www.cultureczars.com/resources.

Now that you've finished reading *The Culture Fix*, I'd love to hear what you thought of it! Please share what you liked, disliked, or how this book has helped you and your company. You can do this by writing a review on *The Culture Fix*'s Amazon listing to help other readers find the best book for them. If you'd like to start a conversation, email me directly at will@cultureczars.com.

Connect with Culture Czar Will Scott online via:

LinkedIn: https://www.linkedin.com/in/willjscott/

Twitter: https://twitter.com/WilljrScott

Facebook: https://www.facebook.com/CultureCzars/

Instagram: https://www.instagram.com/culture_czars/

From Core Values To Valued Culture Podcast:
www.cultureczars.com/podcasts

Corporate Culture Blog:
https://www.cultureczars.com/company-culture-ideas-blog

About the Author

Will Scott is passionate about creating environments where people thrive so they can be the best that they can be. As the original Culture Czar, Will has studied, researched, and adopted corporate culture strategies in his own companies and helped numerous businesses and organizations implement their own valued cultures. Each one has its own remarkable story and some are shared within these pages.

Will leads workshops and speaks regularly on the subject of corporate culture using his proprietary 9 Deeds in 90 Days to take organizations from core values to valued cultures. Will hosts the *Valued Culture* podcast and blogs about all things relating to corporate culture. He has spoken all over the world, is a media consultant, frequent guest on other podcasts, and also hosts and facilitates group and corporate retreats for leadership and personal development.

A longtime member of the Entrepreneurs Organization, Will served on the board of EO Chicago, is a founding member of EO Wisconsin, and an EO Accelerator Trainer as well as a 10,000 Small Businesses program facilitator. With an MBA in international business from the University of Southern California, Will has been an entrepreneur for more than twenty years and is an implementer of the Entrepreneurial Operating System®.

Born in Zambia, Will is a European and naturalized U.S. citizen who has lived in six countries and done business in more than fifty. He served in the Royal Marines and led transformations in organizations as diverse as SME companies, student unions, churches, and global charitable foundations. Will is the proud father of Sam and Chloe, an avid fan of National Geographic®, a yoga practitioner/meditator, and a frequent triathlete.

Made in United States
Orlando, FL
10 January 2023

28535238R00115